HOLY COW !

IT'S ME

By

Louis E. Landau, D.V.M.

To Ellie

With All My Love

Acknowledgements -

A big 'heaping' thanks to Steve Larson and _Hoard's Dairyman_ for publishing articles in their magazine. Without Steve's encouragement, this book would not have happened.

Thanks to all of the animal owners whose loyalty and friendship were needed to make the practice a success.

To Ken Curtis, Al Kremer, Bill Skog and all those that are described in this book: I could not have done it without you.

To Adda, Mary Lou, and many other people whose advice and help made being a veterinarian a pleasure.

1

In 1961, Barrington, Illinois was a sleepy, small mid-western village, located about 30 miles west of Chicago and about to explode into suburban sprawl. The community was very affluent. Mansions were nestled in beautiful forested rolling hills surrounded by huge estates with long paved driveways. Many of these 'ranches' were home to industrialists and wealthy businessmen. The barns on these estates housed some of the best horses in America. A few dairy farms still existed but they were being swallowed by urban development.

My first job as a graduate veterinarian was with Dr. William Bauman of Barrington. I had interned with Dr. Harold Bonner the previous summer. Dr. Bonner had heard that Dr. Bauman was looking for another veterinarian to work in his practice, and he recommended me.

I was hired to be the third veterinarian in his predominately equine practice that also catered to the few remaining dairy herds in the area. Over time, the countryside had changed from dairies and cows to stables and horses. Dr. Bauman had adjusted his practice to accommodate the changes.

Dr. Bauman was in his middle fifties with short gray hair, deep blue eyes, and a very craggy face. A horse had kicked him causing extensive damage to his head that required a lot of surgery. He was about 5'10" tall, wiry, and thin. He suffered from gastric ulcers and was constantly swallowing antacid pills.

Dr. Bob Fetzner was second in command. He was tall, over six feet, well built, and strong. His brown, trimmed hair set off a handsome square face. Bob, in his early thirties, had practiced with Dr. Bauman for more than seven years. Bob, his attractive wife, Karen, and three children lived in Wauconda, Illinois, a small town about 10 miles north of Barrington. Wauconda was built around a lake, and the Fetzners owned a home on the beach.

Dr. Bauman's wife, Gwen, ran the practice from her home by fielding calls. She distributed the calls to the veterinarians in their cars. Each car had a mobile radio, which was the latest in technology in those days.

Gwen was a tall, thin woman, in her late forties or early fifties and enjoyed being in command. Into this mix came I, the rookie, with no knowledge of what to do in practice. All I had was a lot of years of classes and limited intern experience. I lacked confidence and felt inferior to these intelligent, experienced, veterinarians who had developed a thriving practice.

I was 25 years old, rather tall, about six feet two inches, and had been overweight most of my life. I have long legs and a short neck. I inherited a receding hairline from my father. My head is large, and I have difficulty purchasing hats. Usually, the 'large' size is too small. I have bushy eyebrows, hazel eyes and wear glasses to correct my nearsightedness.

Dr. Bauman owned an apartment building in Lake Zurich, a town about 6 miles from Barrington. The building was a converted school, and part of my compensation was the use of the apartment. It had hardwood floors, two bedrooms, a large living and dining room combination, and a very small kitchen with a stove and refrigerator. I did not own furniture, so I slept on the floor. Parking was in the rear of the building where the school playground had been. This was my first residence as a graduate veterinarian. It was luxurious compared to the campus apartments I had lived in during my college days.

Lake Zurich was a resort town for middle-income city dwellers who lived in nearby Chicago. Its main street runs east and west skirting the lake that gave the city its name.

The main street had a hotel, a bank, a grocery store, and a few antique shops. A large drugstore on the corner was humming with business. Many evenings, I would walk to the drug store and visit with the pharmacist. Barrington, Wauconda, and Lake Zurich were about equal in size, each with a population of about 3,000. No one at the time could predict that the entire area would become a vast suburb, and the local flavor of each community lost in the sprawl.

The first few weeks were uneventful. As the rookie in the practice, I rode with Dr. Bauman to many horse clients, did the lab-work in Bill's basement, and spent a lot of time doing records and paperwork. The patients we visited on our rounds were often unruly and obnoxious. My job was to restrain them so that Bill could examine and treat them. The burden of holding these animals shifted from the owner to me. Most patients realized that I didn't show fear and were cooperative.

The lab-work consisted of looking for intestinal worms in fecal samples and counting blood cells. Horses are prone to worm infestations. The severity and identity of the parasite can be established by seeing the eggs with a microscope. Higher than normal white cells meant an infection would be present and a lower than normal red cells indicated anemia. Nothing in the lab was automated and formulas for doing the work were meticulous. Erroneous results were common

No one liked doing records and paperwork. The job was mine by default. There were not any computers, and everything had to be written in long hand. I was responsible for writing the bills as dictated to me and keeping the files on patients. I was bored. I wanted to work directly with the animals.

Most veterinarians hate working nights and weekends. Emergencies can be very draining. I knew my turn would come, because Bill and Bob were getting tired. I was excited, and at the same time, terrified. This was the opportunity I had been waiting for, trained for, and dreaded.

One of my first weekends on call was a glorious Sunday. An emergency obstetrical case was called in to our weekend phone service. One of Bill's relatives had a cow trying to have a calf, but something was wrong. "Right up my alley," I thought.

"I'll be right there," I said upon receiving the message.

I pulled into the driveway and headed toward the barn where the farmer awaited me. Since I had been on this farm with Bill, the farmer was aware I was the new veterinarian.

"Isn't Bill or Bob available?" the farmer asked.

"No," I replied, somewhat disappointed in my reception.

"Alright then," he said. "I'll show you where she is."

The farmer, wearing the bib blue jeans uniform of most dairymen, led the way. I followed him, carrying the equipment I would need. When we arrived at the pen, I noticed an obvious smirk on the farmer's face.

It didn't matter what the farmer thought, I was actually going to work on a cow without one of the other veterinarians looking over my shoulder and giving me advice.

The cow was lying in a clean, comfortable stall, and I could see the tail of the calf protruding from the vulva. No feet just tail. The calf was in a breech position. Cows normally calve feet first. I needed to have the cow stand so I could push the calf forward and reach a leg, but no matter what we tried, the cow refused to get up.

I went inside her vagina to check the condition of the calf, and to my dismay, found that the calf was already dead. It was starting to swell and smell. Now, I had to concentrate on saving the cow.

Lying on my stomach, with my hand and arm in the cow, was the only way to reach the calf to manipulate it. As I worked, fluids trapped in the uterus spilled over me. I was getting sticky, wet, and uncomfortable. The odor of dead tissue made the farmer gag.

"So what are you finding?" he asked with a grin.

"A dead swollen calf that really stinks," I answered.

"Kinda figured that," he replied. "Where did Bill say he was going?"

I ignored the question and was determined to remove this calf without any help from Bill.

The only way to save the cow was to cut the dead calf into smaller pieces. Finally, I was able to hook umbilical wire around a leg and hip. Moving the wire back and forth would cut off that leg and hip. To protect the cow, I placed a metal tube inside the vagina and ran the wire through it, tied a handle to each end of the wire and had the owner pull the handles back and forth, which resulted in sawing through the calf.

My conversation was now limited to directions and grunts. I removed the part of the calf that we had sawed. Now I had access to the remainder of the calf. I reach back into the cow and extracted the rest of the calf. I was exhausted, dirty, smelly, and wet.

One of my professors in school said to always check a cow for another calf, just to be sure that she wasn't trying to deliver twins. Again, I reached inside the cow and there, to my disbelief, was another calf.

Did I have enough strength to get this one out too? I would try. Again, I was behind the cow on my stomach. The second calf was much smaller than the first one. I delivered it without any major difficulty.

I was greatly relieved, and so was the cow. She looked around, got up, and started to eat. As I watched her, I felt the joy of accomplishment, and the knowledge that I had passed an important test. I felt a high that would repeat many times during my long career. I had chosen a profession that helps distressed animals. I had the contentment of knowing it was the right one for me. Years later, I would find a much easier way to deliver breech calves, but this was my first case.

I had spent three hours working on those calves. Several days later, the farmer approached Bill and complained that I had taken too much of his time. Bill asked about the condition of the cow.

"Oh, now she is one of my best cows," he said.

"Then quit bitching" Bill said. The farmer thought it over and agreed with Dr. Bauman that I had done a good job.

2

I met Ellie on a blind date in college at the University of Illinois. I was immediately attracted by her beauty and intelligence. Ellie is petite at 5 feet 3 inches. Her sparkling, big, black eyes captured me from the start. Her black hair surrounded a round face with a button nose perfectly sculptured for her face. When she smiled and laughed, the world became a happy place for me.

We were engaged for over a year, and now, that I had a job, and an apartment (unfurnished) we were going to be married. Our wedding took place at O'Have Sholem Synagogue in Rockford, Illinois, on September 3rd, 1961.

The day was brutally hot, and the synagogue wasn't air-conditioned. The sanctuary, which was on the second floor, was stifling. Two rabbis conducted the service. The rabbi of the congregation co-officiated with the rabbi that had led the congregation when Ellie was a teenager. Each rabbi offered his lengthy words of wisdom and advice as the sweat dripped down my back. We said our vows under the *chupah*, the traditional Jewish wedding canopy.

A large reception was held in the social hall of the synagogue. After that, we left for a short honeymoon, and then headed to Lake Zurich to start our life together.

Ellie was now the wife of a farm veterinarian. To learn more, she would ride with me to the farms and watch as I treated sick animals. I loved to have her with me, but soon she was bored, just as I had been when I was riding with Bill.

One day, we received a call from a stable that had a horse with colic or a severe stomachache. The pain of colic is so bad that horses tend to kick out without warning. They might roll on the ground, which can create twists in the gut. If not treated, a horse in with colic might injure itself, other animals or people. Treatment consists of painkillers, muscle relaxants, and a gallon of mineral oil pumped into the stomach using a stomach tube.

When I went to take care of my patient, the stable owner's wife gave Ellie a tour of the farm. The stable hands were preparing a stallion to breed a mare. Since this was not a 'proper' thing for young ladies to observe, the stable owner's wife tried to direct Ellie's attention to some other features of the stables. Politely, Ellie followed her hostess away from the breeding area of the stables. She was not happy that those puritan ideas prevented her from watching a normal, routine procedure.

I had borrowed money from my parents to buy furniture for our apartment. We bought the bare essentials, a bedroom set, living room pieces, an ugly rug (because it was cheap), and a kitchen table and chairs.

Since money was scarce, Ellie decided to find office work. She had several interviews. One company had her take an aptitude test, which she passed with ease. During her interview with the personnel manager, she was told she did extremely well on the aptitude test, but the company could not afford to invest time and money to train a young married woman. "After all," she was told, "you *might* get pregnant."

About a month later, that company did call Ellie with a job offer. She felt she had to be truthful and decline the position because now, she was pregnant. Attitudes and affirmative action laws dealing with the hiring of women have changed for the better since 1961.

3

The more work I was allowed to do on my own, the more confident I became. One weekend, I responded to a horse owner's frantic, emergency call for assistance with a choking mare. Feeling pretty cocky, I drove there planning my attack on the problem. It had to be a foreign object lodged in the horse's esophagus. I would simply pass a tube down its throat, move the object, and I would be a hero.

A very worried owner met me at the horse barn. "I've never seen a horse doing this," Jack Bartell said.

"No problem," I assured him.

He took me to the horse. The animal was having trouble breathing as he had described over the phone. Since I had assumed that there was a foreign object lodged in the neck, I whipped out my stomach tube, a black plastic or rubber tube much like a hose, and passed it down the horse's neck. There wasn't any of the expected resistance. Something was wrong with my assumption.

I stepped back for a better look and realized that the reason for the horse's apparent choking was due to the horse pressing its neck against a board.

"Let's move the horse," I suggested. We tried to push the horse, but it would not budge.

The horse wasn't suffering from a choke caused by a foreign body. He had symptoms of brain damage. My mind raced with a possible diagnosis. Horses develop encephalitis or brain infections from different causes. The most prevalent reason is a viral infection. Some of these viral infections are contagious to man.

"Rabies!" I thought feeling devastated. I was too scared to blurt it out. I had my hand covered with contaminated saliva. The rabies virus is transmitted from animals to humans through infected saliva. Rabies can be fatal. Not only had I been exposed, but also, while helping me, the owner had been exposed.

"I have made a terrible mistake," I told Jack. He was stunned at my diagnosis, and I was shocked by my stupidity. My newly achieved self-confidence was shattered.

I went back early the next morning hoping the horse would have improved. No such luck. It had died. "I have to cut off the head and take it to a lab to get an exact diagnosis," I told Jack.

I wrapped the head in plastic and put it in the front seat of my car. I drove straight to the lab, which was about 30 minutes away in downtown Chicago. I did not trust anyone else to transport such a potential deadly object.

The diagnosis would not be known for ten days. This was a time of extreme self-doubt. I questioned everything, including why had I gone to veterinary school. I had exposed Jack because he had helped me.

Finally, the lab results came back. The horse had died of a viral infection that was NOT rabies and was NOT contagious to humans. Jubilantly, I called Jack with the good news. "I wasn't that worried," he said happily. "While I have you on the phone, can you worm a horse for me this afternoon?" he asked.

"Sure," I responded. I felt that Jack had more confidence in my work than I did. I vowed never again to treat an animal without first evaluating the entire situation. I would never endanger another human life again.

4

The mansions around Barrington were surrounded by farmland. The land would be sold to developers who built elegant houses. These homes were sold to people who moved out to the country to get away from the city. They became 'gentlemen farmers' and bought horses.

When a horse needs veterinary care, the owner must be able to restrain it. Horses are strong and may weigh over 1000 pounds. One way to make a horse stand still is to use a twitch on the horse's nose. The twitch is a handle with a chain or rope fastened on one end. The idea is to have the horse focus on the pain in the nose rather than on the area needing the examination. The end of a horse's nose is placed inside the loop of chain or rope, and the handle is twisted. This process causes pain. The harder the handle is twisted the more pain is experienced. It is often the only way an unruly horse allows an exam of a painful area.

To an inexperienced person, it seems as though the animal is being injured. Horses that are routinely twitched, do not object. A little nose rub after removing the twitch is all that is required to relieve the pain.

I was called to check a pony with sore ears. A woman, who was 8 months pregnant, greeted me. As I followed her into the stable, I asked, "Is there someone who can help me hold the pony?"

"I will hold her for you. That's why I'm here," she answered indignantly.

The pony was undisciplined and did not like being

12

touched. I tried to examine the ear, but each time I got close, the pony pulled back. I needed the twitch. The pony kept moving, and was extremely uncooperative. With great effort, I secured the instrument and apprehensively gave the handle to the woman. I did not have any confidence in her ability to use it correctly.

"Keep the twitch tight, so the pony will stand still. Then, I can examine the ear." I explained.

Instead of retaining pressure and 'hurting' the horse, she released the tension. Experiencing no more pain, the pony reared, throwing the woman into the air and against a wall. I ran over to help, unsure of the extent of her injuries. Fortunately, she got up, brushed herself off and said, "Let's continue."

"No," I said. "Let's not." I wasn't going through that again. With that comment, I left.

I explained the situation to Bill, and he agreed that I had done the right thing. However, the husband called later that day berating me for leaving without treating the pony. Bill gave him a lecture about how unrestrained animals can cause human injury.

I examined the pony again, but this time I had qualified help. A fungus had grown in the pony's ear and was easily identified when the animal was properly restrained. I didn't see the pony again. It either improved or was sold.

5

When business was slow, Bill liked me to ride with him. I would pick up some practical experience and help with restraining the animals. One day, when Bill and I were making rounds, he apologetically told me the practice could not afford a third veterinarian.

"Perhaps you should be looking elsewhere," he suggested.

I had just been fired. I was stunned. I was married, expecting a child, and now, I no longer had a job. My mind was reeling.

Suddenly, the car lurched, and I focused on the road. Bill was passing a gravel truck. The truck driver slowed, did not see us, and started to turn left into a driveway. We were caught between the truck and a ditch. Bill turned the car so we were up against the truck as it turned, metal on metal. The truck driver was still oblivious to any problem. The two vehicles were turning as one. Finally the truck stopped.

We were jostled and badly shaken, but not hurt. The practice car received a lot of damage. The accident must have triggered Bill to have some soul searching thoughts. While we were waiting for a tow truck, he turned to me and said he had reconsidered his comment prior to the accident. He wanted me to stay and continue working for him. I was relieved, but had an ominous feeling that I had not heard his last word on the topic.

The car was not totaled but had sustained enough damage to require at least 3 to 4 weeks for repair. Bill didn't want to wait that long and bought a new car.

Bill always bought 2 door Chevrolet coupes. The back seats were taken out and replaced with wooden boxes that held our instruments. When the wrecked one was repaired, it would be mine to drive. My first practice car would be a 1959 brown Chevrolet coupe.

My confidence in my abilities was growing, once again. I was practicing good medicine, and I felt very comfortable. I was developing my own clientele. They wanted me, and would accept Bob or Bill only in an emergency.

A farmer called our office asking for a veterinarian to help with a lame cow. Bill told me to take this one on my own. I didn't think I would be challenged on a call like that.

I had never heard of this particular client. With directions in hand, I jumped in my car and was off to tackle the problem.

A thickly bearded old man with extremely dirty clothes came out to greet me. "What would a young fellow like you know about cows?" he asked. He informed me that over the years he had seen everything and knew all there was to know.

I asked, "Why did you call the office for help with a lame cow?"

He replied, "I need someone to hold the rope."

Why not, I thought to myself. I'm already here. I got a rope out of the trunk of the car and went into the barn. As I lifted the foot, the old man admitted he couldn't tell what was causing the lameness.

I went back to my car for instruments. I cleaned the foot, found an abscess, opened it, and relieved the pain. I must have really impressed the old guy, because he asked me to look at two cows by his hay barn. It was above the holding stalls where his cows were tied.

I was stunned to find two comatose cows lying in the driveway of the hayloft, barely breathing. "How long have these animals been here in this state?" I questioned.

"About three days" he replied.

"Why didn't you call to have these cows examined?" I asked in wonderment.

"Didn't want to waste the money because there isn't nothing you can do for them anyway. They might as well be dead," he managed to say around a big wad of chewing tobacco.

"When did they have their calves," I asked.

"A few days before going down," he replied.

Could this be simple milkfever or eclampsia? Milkfever is a common problem with dairy cows after calving. As milk is starting to be produced in the udder, the demand for calcium is increased. If too much calcium is taken from the blood stream, the cow can go down or even lose consciousness. The lowered calcium causes nerves to become unresponsive.

Milkfever is always handled as an emergency. Cows can't survive very long without treatment. These two cows had been down for three days. I needed to administer a calcium I.V. drip into the jugular vein of each cow. If the calcium helped these cows, then, my initial diagnosis of milkfever was correct.

I went back to the car for intravenous tubing and calcium. A dairy practitioner always carries many bottles of calcium to have for this kind of emergency.

I prepared my treatments carefully and proceeded to find the vein in the cow I felt was closest to death. Even though there was very little blood pressure, I managed to find the vein.

Now I had to control the flow of the calcium. Calcium is tricky to administer, because it can cause a heart attack if allowed to run too rapidly or if the animal has a heart condition.

Fearlessly, I continued with my therapy, I had nothing to lose. To my amazement the cow began to stir. I continued treatment. She started blinking her eyes and picked up her head. I gave her the full bottle and then started the procedure on the second cow. She responded as well.

By about now the old man's tobacco chew was running down the stubble on his chin. I was as shocked as he was. In a little while, both cows got to their feet and were looking for something to eat.

I can't describe the feeling. Using modern medicine, I was able to bring two dying cows back to life. This 'miracle', with the accompanying feeling of amazement, would repeat many times during my career, but this was my first time.

When I handed the astonished client the bill for services, he was very willing to pay. "I really got my money's worth!" he commented. I lectured him on the need for veterinary care and told him to call more often. He thanked me and assured me we would see much more of him. We never saw him again.

As the weeks went by, my job with Bill and Bob was becoming more insecure. It seemed that after a few slow days, Bill would call me in and tell me the practice could not afford three full time veterinarians, and I should start looking for a different position. A few days later, he would say that he had reconsidered, and I was welcome to stay. The more Bill fired and rehired me, the more I became convinced I needed to start looking for another place to work.

6

Bill's indecision about my job could go on indefinitely. I had to break the cycle. I determined I had three alternatives. I could work in another veterinary practice, I could buy an established practice, or I could 'hang out a shingle' and set up my own practice.

I started looking at veterinary want ads. There were many positions available, but I might end up being asked to leave again. Ellie and I visited a few practices that were for sale. I was willing to pay for the tangible items like equipment and a building, but I wasn't willing to pay additional money for an intangible client list, commonly referred to as 'blue sky'. The best alternative, and my ultimate dream, was to start my own practice. The major drawback was money.

I explained my dilemma to my father. He offered me an interest free loan. I bought a new 1961 Nash Rambler for $2,000, which would be my practice vehicle. I didn't know where I was going to locate, but I was prepared.

Late in the spring, Bill asked to talk to me. I knew he was going to give me the 'business is slow" speech.

This time I made the opening statement. "I am planning on leaving. My position here is too unstable. I want a practice of my own," I told him.

I don't know why, but he was surprised. He wanted me to stay long enough for him to go on an extended vacation. Ellie was 8 months pregnant, so I agreed to stay until the end of September with time off to find a place of my own.

Father's Day, 1962, turned out to be a beautiful, bright, sunny day with a promise of wonderful things to come. Ellie's family had planned to come to Lake Zurich to spend the day with us, but Ellie went into labor. I was on call that day, so I immediately phoned Bill about my wonderful news. "Take all the time you need," he said.

Deborah Sue Landau was born at 10 p.m. on June 17th. Mother and daughter were both fine, and I was bursting with love and happiness.

Ellie and Debbie came home from the hospital after five days. I had assembled the crib and organized all the baby supplies. It was an exciting time. However, in the back of my mind, I was concerned about my work problems. Could I start a practice on my own?

The answer to my question came from Bill although he never knew it. He took a long vacation to Alaska leaving Bob and me to run the practice. Bob already had five years of experience and had confidence in my abilities. He didn't question my judgments or decisions and let me practice in my own way.

I began making 20 calls a day, and the more I worked, the better I became. I knew that I was a very capable practitioner, and people were respecting me for my knowledge and animal expertise. I had proven to myself that I was able to do the job.

Where to go was still undecided. I totally ruled out working for someone else. Buying an established practice did not seem feasible. I had to find a place to set up my own practice with the desire to be successful, as my only asset. Quite a challenge.

My father was a cattle buyer in Holland before immigrating to the United States. He found he could do the same kind of work in this country.

During his search to buy cows for resale, Dad mentioned to a farmer, my desire to set up a veterinary practice. The farmer suggested Shullsburg, Wisconsin, a small town about 45 minutes from my parents' farm. The farmer had heard the veterinarian who lived in Shullsburg had health problems and wasn't able to practice full time.

Dad investigated the area and thought he had found the town for our future. It was remote with few people but there were many farms with dairy cows. After seeing Shullsburg and talking to people, I too, thought it would be a perfect place to set up a veterinary practice.

7

The same sun that warms Barrington, Illinois, shines above Shullsburg, Wisconsin, but the similarity ends there. Barrington is urban, and Shullsburg is rural. Traffic is non-existent in Shullsburg. There aren't any traffic lights in the entire county. The water is so pure each gulp is refreshing.

The land north and west of Shullsburg is fertile, level, and deep. Land south and west of Shullsburg is more rugged and beautiful. Lead, copper, zinc, and silver were mined in this area.

Shullsburg was one of the first settlements in Wisconsin. The mines attracted immigrant settlers. Tunnels created to extract the "gray gold" undermine the city.

One large lead-mine was operational when we moved here in 1962. Large ore trucks would disappear into the mine entrance. They would be driven underground to the work area. The trucks would come back to the surface filled with mineral laden rocks. The residue that remained after the minerals were extracted from these rocks is called tailings. The area south and west of Shullsburg is punctuated with huge piles of tailings.

Shullsburg is 8 miles north of the Illinois border and 30 miles east of the Mississippi River, which borders eastern Iowa. Dubuque, Iowa, is the closest 'large' city. This southwest corner of Wisconsin has been undiscovered and is a wonderful place to call home.

I came here to work and raise a family, unaware of the friendly, helpful people, the beautiful scenery, and the relaxed pace of living a small rural agricultural and mining community had to offer.

We moved to an apartment above Alt's Plumbing store located on Water Street, the main street that ran through the center of town. From the street behind the building, a suspended wooden walkway led to the entrance of the second floor apartment.

The view from the front room windows of the apartment captured the downtown buildings that had been built in the 1800's. Those buildings are now part of Shullsburg's historic downtown district.

I rented a storefront on Water Street, two blocks east of our apartment. It served as an office and a clinic. I hung out my shingle and was ready to start my own practice.

Could my dream of owning a practice be coming true? There would be a few hurdles to overcome and unexpected turns. Nothing is as easy as it seems.

I wanted to introduce myself to other veterinarians in the area. In Barrington, veterinarians in the neighboring practices were friends and colleagues. I wanted that same feeling to exist here.

My first visit was to Dr. Douglas Whitehall. Dr. Whitehall was somewhat responsible for me being in Shullsburg. After Dad had suggested Shullsburg as an area needing a veterinarian, I had called Dr. Whitehall on the phone. I told him I was looking for a place to work. When he found out what I wanted, he became very defensive and hung up the phone. That made me curious and interested in Shullsburg, otherwise, I may not have even considered moving here.

Dr. Whitehall was the most prominent veterinarian in town. His office was also on Water Street. It was three blocks from my rented store front and about a block from our apartment. His office was on the main floor of a corner building, and his living quarters were on the second floor.

I walked in and introduced myself. "So, you're the one who opened an office up the street," he said as he turned away from me. "I will keep all the clients I have," was all he said to me. With that, he disappeared into a back room.

"Wow," I thought. He sure wasn't friendly or polite. I was young and naïve and didn't realize I was seen as a competitor not a colleague.

Next, I went to visit the retired veterinarian in town, Dr. George Tyson. He had spent the better part of his career in government service. I told him of my last encounter. "That don't surprise me none," he said. He smiled and promised to tell his friends and relatives to call me for their veterinary work. He was pleasant and helpful, but I wasn't a threat to him.

I visited a neighboring town and a third veterinarian. Darlington, Wisconsin, is about 12 miles northeast of Shullsburg. With the miles between us, I thought a neighboring practice would surely welcome me.

Dr. James Bleu questioned why I had come to Shullsburg and commented that I should go somewhere else. He didn't like having me set up another practice in his 'backyard'.

I hadn't expected to be treated so rudely. A few months later, I found that there were veterinarians in other neighboring communities that would have welcomed me. Most of them were extremely busy with more work than they could handle and would have welcomed some relief.

8

My main interest in veterinary school had been in food animal medicine. I focused my attention in that area more than in companion animal medicine. However, I needed work and would treat any animal.

My first case in my new office involved a dog. The dog had been run over by a car and had a broken leg. The dog needed a Thomas splint. This device is used to stretch the leg and immobilize it. It looks like a permanent crutch attached to the hip.

The femur was broken, and by stretching and pulling, I was able to connect the broken ends so healing could occur. With the Thomas splint on the leg, I sent the dog home.

He was a farm dog, owned by a family that lived close to town. The owners were very appreciative of the care I gave the dog, and they promised to call for assistance with their food animal work.

Every time I made a visit to the farm, the dog would greet me with a cacophony of barking, his way of saying hello. One time, I noticed the splint was getting loose, but I didn't think it would cause any problems. I concentrated on treating the cows in the barn.

The splint finally worked itself off, leaving the dog with a crooked leg. The dog didn't seem to notice. His owner, Dennis Leibold, didn't seem to care, but I noticed and felt embarrassed.

I made frequent calls to that farm, and the dog always welcomed me. He lived to be very old, and when he died, I mourned him. My repair job might not have been perfect, but it gave the dog the opportunity to survive and live a long and happy life. Besides, it was ammunition for Dennis to ridicule me. "Remember that dog," he would say with a big grin.

My very first farm call was a disaster. Ted Kessler, a pig farmer, called the office asking for help with baby pig scours or diarrhea. I had treated this kind of problem in Barrington. An injection of antibiotics cured the pigs.

I started injecting the pigs in an assembly line fashion. Ted and his sons would grab a pig, hold it up, and I would walk up and down in front of them 'shooting' each pig. I paused in the sequence to look back at the pigs that I had already treated. "Oh @#$%," I yelled. "These pigs are in shock!"

I ran to my truck for the antihistamines to counter the reaction, but for many pigs, it was too late. They were allergic to the solution that was used to carry the antibiotic. This allergic reaction was a constant problem in the early years of my practice. Currently, products are more refined and safe, and shock is a minor side effect.

The farmer took the loss quite well, but I was very distressed. I was so disgusted with the product that once outside the pig house, I hurled the bottle as far as I could throw it. I should have been smarter and not acted so irrationally.

I complained to the manufacturer, but wasn't able to get any satisfactory explanation. They told me they needed to test the contents of the bottle before they would admit to any problem. I could not find the bottle that I had flung in my rage. The beginning of my own practice was off to a shaky start.

Jim Reilly, a Surge milk machine dealer, asked if I was interested in a class on milk machine function. It would be held at Surge's home office in Chicago. Jim offered to pay my tuition and some of my expenses.

I thought I should stay in Shullsburg and be available for calls, but Ellie convinced me to go. She would answer the phone and schedule work upon my return. The special planning wasn't necessary. Not a single call came in when I was attending the class.

I was getting discouraged. I wasn't making enough money to pay the bills or pay my father, who lent us money to buy the car and supplies. He had also loaned me an additional $500 to pay for food and rent. I owed him $4,500 and had no way to pay him back.

I was too embarrassed to ask Dad for more money. I felt like a failure. I was getting depressed. I needed more money and decided to apply for a loan at the local bank.

The Farmers and Merchants Bank old building looked like a structure out of the old West. It was located on the corner lot about a block from my office. The cashiers worked in cages behind metal grates. The vault was behind the cages, and from all appearances, Jesse James could enter at any moment.

Tall tables for preparing transactions were along one wall. Customers formed a line along side the tables waiting their turn to speak to the tellers.

Tippy Dole was president, and any loans would need to be approved by him. I asked for $500.00. Since I didn't have collateral, I was turned down on the spot. My DVM degree and my willingness to work hard was not enough security for the old, conservative banker.

I had to fall back on the generosity of my father. I promised him this would be the last time. If I ran out of money, I would leave Shullsburg and find a job working for another veterinarian. Instead of ridiculing me, he encouraged me and told me not to be so hard on myself.

He lent me another $500.00, which bought me a few more months to attempt to create a viable veterinary practice.

The time had come to leave the apartment and find a more permanent home. A Lustron house, a house made entirely of metal, was available. It was constructed of metal panels that had a glass like glaze on the outside surface. The inside wall was baked enamel with a hideous brown color that could not be changed. I was told that it was hot in summer and cold in winter.

The house was located across from the municipal swimming pool in Badger Park. Shullsburg's pool and park were built by WPA during the depression of the 1930's. Before that, the park had been an old mining site, which had been pocked by mining holes leaving a scarred surface.

I was getting desperate and discouraged. Since professional advertising was unethical in those days, I needed to find a way to attract clients. We had enough money to pay the rent for a few more months, and then, if business didn't improve, we would have to leave.

9

The State of Wisconsin was administrating a tuberculosis eradication program on dairy cows and contracting local veterinarians to do the testing. The program was intended to eliminate human exposure to tuberculosis and was processed at no cost to the owners of the cows.

A state-employed veterinarian came to Shullsburg to teach me how to give intradermal injections. This type of injection places the drugs in the layers of the skin.

Tuberculin is an antigen or foreign protein, and when given to animals suffering from tuberculosis, the immune system would recognize the antigen, and a lump or swelling would occur. We were required to examine the injection site 72 hours after the antigen was administered. If there was no lump, then it was safe to assume the animal tested negative, which meant it did not have TB. If any cow over two years old tested positive, it had to be slaughtered

The tuberculin was injected where the tail connects to the body of the cow. The veterinarian had to stand directly behind the rear feet of the animal to give the injection. I had to stay alert, because some cows chose to use those feet to kick at the annoying 'thing' at her tail.

I was assigned certain townships in the county and stopped by the farms to make an appointment for the TB testing. The farmers had to find time to make their cows available to me. Scheduling the testing was met with a lot of grumbling, because it added work to their already busy schedule. However, those farmers that did not comply could be fined and be legally forced to have their cows tested.

Human TB is a deadly, debilitating disease that often affects the lungs. A TB lesion is a round granulating ball that keeps increasing in size. Inside the lesion is a pocket, which is filled with dried pus like substance. One of the main symptoms in people with TB is a chronic cough. TB sanitariums were built to care for patients suffering from the disease. Cows and humans shared the TB organism, and if the disease could be controlled in cows, then humans would have less exposure. By the time that I started practice, few, if any, TB was diagnosed in cows.

Doing the TB testing for the state of Wisconsin gave me a reason to visit farms, meet prospective clients, and make some money.

I followed a map and found farms on roads I never knew existed. Once, I found a farm so isolated that I had to open numerous gates, go over rocks and bumps, and generally abuse my little Rambler to get there. I told the farmer what I wanted, and requested an appointment. With much reluctance, he consented.

He told me to bring a restraining chute to test the heifers that were out in the pasture. This would require my Rambler to pull a heavy trailer over this rough terrain. I went back the same way, wondering how a milk truck negotiated this lane, particularly in snow and ice

A week later, I went back and tested the cows. When I was getting ready to leave, I observed secretive smiles and side-glances between the farmer and the men who were there to help. Later, I learned there was a good road that went right up to the farmstead. It was relatively new and was not on my map. Since the farmer really didn't want to do the testing, he didn't tell me of the more direct way to get to his farm.

Most of the farmers were very cooperative, because they had friends or relatives that had contracted TB from cows. Identifying and slaughtering the infected cows helped reduce the chances of family members getting sick.

The testing procedure ran quite smoothly. Each animal had to be identified with a metal ear tag. Clamping the tag was the most difficult part of the process. After the 3 day waiting period, I went back to feel for lumps at the injection site. If I didn't feel anything suspicious, I would give the farmer a form that stated his cows all tested negative.

During the testing phase, the farmers and I would start up a conversation. They were curious about me, the new veterinarian in Shullsburg. They asked why I had decided to come to this area. Many of them would ask for my phone number, and I was thrilled to give it to them.

Slowly, I was building a nucleus of clients. During the ensuing 36 years of practice, I did veterinary work for many of these farmers and continued to work for the next generation, when their children took over the farms.

The testing program by the state was discontinued after that first year I was in Shullsburg. I had found only one animal who was a suspect of having TB. When I retested her, the results were negative.

Was the program successful? It was a very expensive survey for the state. However, it showed that the testing performed in previous years was very effective in making these herds have a very low incidence of TB.

There is still some tuberculosis in wildlife and in other countries, but human TB sanitariums in the United States are no longer prevalent.

10

We did not need all of the $500.00 I had borrowed from Dad the second time. I was making enough money to start repaying him.

Bob Trost was a great help in the early days of my practice. He bought and sold feeder pigs. My Dad had met Bob at animal auctions, which they both attended. Since Bob didn't live far from Shullsburg, Dad suggested that he call me for his veterinary work.

Federal law, at the time, required pigs to receive cholera vaccinations before they could be moved from one farm to another. Two injections were necessary. One injection contained a slightly modified virus, and the other one contained the antiserum that would kill the virus. Each pig had to be caught, and each injection had to be administered in a different place on the pig. The purpose of these injections was to give the pig a mild case of cholera so it could build up immunity against the killer disease. Male pigs were often castrated at the same time.

Bob would call and ask me to come to his farm and vaccinate pigs. He didn't demand immediate service, but I always tried to be there early the next morning. Having productive work was a great way to start the day. I am grateful to Bob for the role he played in my success.

Even though the government required pigs to be vaccinated against cholera, the virus was not eradicated and outbreaks continued to occur. Research veterinarians concluded the vaccine was the main cause of the cholera outbreaks. The law requiring vaccinations was reversed in the late 1960's, and use of the vaccine was outlawed. The United States is now free of cholera.

I had been in practice for about six months when Ernie Hendrickson, Sr. called to say he had a cow that had a prolapsed uterus. "Would you please come and help her?" Ernie asked over the phone. He lived about two miles south of Shullsburg, and I had admired his farm every time I passed it.

The sun was just setting as I pulled in. A spry old man with an easy smile and a warm handshake met me at his barn. He showed me the cow, and I knew I was in trouble.

Her uterus and cervix were completely eviscerated, or turned inside out, and were hanging outside of her body. To make matters worse, the uterus was very swollen. It had increased in size from fitting into a 10-gallon pail to a mass larger than a bushel basket. The caruncles, which are the large button like placental attachment areas, were dripping with blood. To replace and return the uterus is hard work under the best of circumstances, but this one was going to be a real challenge.

I gave the cow a caudal epidural to stop her from straining and pushing, but it was only partially successful. We had to hold up the uterus so it would be higher then the vulva, then force it back through the vagina, and twist it into its correct position. Every time we got close to replacing it, the cow would strain and push it out again, and we would have to start from the beginning of the process.

I passed a stomach tube down her throat to prevent further straining but the cow continued to push. She became tired after two hours, and we were able to replace the uterus and stitch the vulva closed.

Ernie and I were exhausted. We sat on a bale of

hay resting from the strenuous effort. The cow was feeling much better and eating everything in sight.

"I appreciate what you did for me tonight," Ernie said. "I thought you would give up and quit."

I had thought about it, but the cow would have died. "Nope, this is part of my job," I said.

The sun had set long ago, and it was quite dark when I got back into my car. I enjoyed talking to Ernie. His family would become very involved with the practice I was starting. I had made a good friend and client.

11

Ellie was the office manager. "Roger Reynolds, a new client from Warren Illinois, called," she said when I phoned her to check in. "He has two cows locked in stanchions in a holding area next to his milking parlor. They both have udder infections. Treat them and turn them out. No one will be at home."

I had never met Roger, yet he wanted his cows treated without anyone available to help or to give me additional information. This was unusual.

I drove to the farm and found the cows in the barn as Ellie had said. I gave them both an intravenous treatment. I left a note for Roger explaining the diagnosis and the treatment I had given to them. Several days later he called again. He had some different cows to treat, but they had the same problem, mastitis.

"No one is home so release the cows when finished," was written on a note attached to the barn door. A few days later, he repeated the same scenario.

The next time I went to his farm, he was there. Roger had heard me drive up and came out of the barn. This was the first time I had met him. "You're no better then the rest of the vets I have had," was his first comment. "All you do is treat the cows, but don't fix the problem," he said.

"I was told to treat the cows, and let them out," I answered defensively.

"I am going broke because my cows continue to get mastitis and aren't giving enough milk. I can't find anyone to help, including you," he retorted angrily.

I told him, when I come to the farm to treat the cows, I need to have someone around who can explain what's going on.

"Well, then, what should I do?" he muttered under his breath.

I explained that his milking equipment needed to be checked, and he should make sure that proper procedures were followed during milking time. As I was describing those procedures, I could see that Roger was becoming irritated. The more I talked the angrier he became. Veins were popping out on his face and neck. He kept clenching and unclenching his hands. He then informed me that he had learned to milk cows from his dad, and he was not about to change. End of conversation.

I headed for my car but before leaving I said, "I'll come back to observe your milking technique." What a dumb thing to say to an angry man. I definitely didn't feel welcome on his farm, but he didn't tell me not to come back. I wasn't sure what I should do.

That night, I told Ellie of my experience and told her I decided not to go back "You have to go back," she said. "You can't help him until you see what he is doing wrong."

I procrastinated as long as I could, but finally went back to Roger's farm. I walked into the milking parlor with clipboard and stopwatch. I talked to no one, and no one talked to me. I watched how a cow was prepped before the milking machine was attached. I timed how long the machine remained on a cow. I observed the general cleanliness of the operation.

Surprisingly, he was doing everything correctly. The procedures he was using would not cause the mastitis. I was confused. Why did this man have such poor milk production from his cows?

I walked over to Roger to apologize for assuming he was not milking correctly. I told him his milking procedure was not the problem. It was something else, but I didn't know what it was.

He apologized to me, also. He explained that after I had left, he was so angry that he could not eat or sleep. While he lay awake in the middle of the night, it occurred to him that I was not trying to insult him, but was actually trying to help him.

He took my advice and had implemented the changes and procedures that I had recommended. He had an equipment dealer correct two major problems with the milking machine. What I was observing was his *new* method of milking his cows.

In less than two months, he tripled his milk production, and now I had a new, satisfied client.

12

Dr. Bauman came to Shullsburg to visit us and to see how things were going. I told him I was happy here, working in my own practice.

Our metal home was not much of an improvement over our apartment in Lake Zurich. My downtown office was unattended and served as storage for my supplies. I showed Bill around Shullsburg and gave him a tour of the surrounding farms and the mining areas.

Bill informed me that shortly after we moved, Bob, my fellow employee, had left the practice in Barrington to go out West. Since Bob had left, Bill had to work longer hours. The extra work was detrimental to his health.

This was the last time I would see Dr. Bauman. He died about a year later. I learned a lot from the practice in Barrington. My experience there gave me the confidence to start my own practice.

While I was driving the Rambler on farm calls, I was preoccupied with my tax bill. An accountant calculated our income tax for our first year in Shullsburg. We owed $500 in taxes. I was shocked. I hadn't made much money that first year and was expecting to owe less than $100. We didn't have enough money to pay $500 in taxes. Suddenly, a 90-degree turn came out of nowhere. I hit the brake, but there was a patch of ice in the curve, and I lost control of the car.

The Rambler started sliding and collided, grill first, with a post that was cemented into the ground. I wasn't hurt, but the damage to the car was so extensive that it could not be driven.

I walked to the closest farmhouse to call a tow truck. The farmer had seen the accident and invited me in to use his phone.

"Say, aren't you that new vet from Shullsburg?" he asked.

"Yes I am," I replied, trying to compose myself.

"Would you mind looking at a sick cow for me? She's been off her feed for a couple of days," he said.

"Sure " I replied. I went back to my wrecked car for my black bag. This was quite an unusual way to introduce myself to a new client.

I did not want to repair the Rambler. I needed a bigger car for making farm calls. I had heard that a car dealership in Monroe, WI, 40 miles east of Shullsburg was offering a lease program. I wasn't happy about the distance I would have to drive for servicing, but car leasing programs were a new marketing ploy, and there were not any dealerships closer to Shullsburg that were promoting the new program.

I made a deal with Alphorn Ford in Monroe to lease a sporty Ford, fully loaded, with a large V8 engine. It was not new, but the few miles on it didn't matter, because the lease covered repairs. I paid for gas, insurance and the monthly fee. The contract did not limit the amount of miles driven, just the number of months I could drive it. My transportation needs had been solved.

One evening, in the middle of winter, a farmer called to have a calf delivered. My parents were visiting, and my father loved accompanying me on calls.

Dad and I bundled up to keep warm. The farm was a considerable distance from Shullsburg, but Dad enjoyed the ride and the chance to visit.

As we stepped from the car, the cold penetrated us. The heifer, my patient, was lying in a large yard surrounded by a foot of soupy manure that was starting to freeze. She was small, malnourished, and could not get up. She was shivering from the cold.

My father, viewing this scene, became upset and irritated. I knew what he was thinking. This poor creature was mistreated and would probably die.

We cleaned the area around the heifer, and since the feet of the calf were protruding from the vulva, I placed chains around the legs and set up the fetal extractor. A brace is placed on the rear end of the mother. A pole and jack are attached to the flat surface of a plate that fits under the vulva providing leverage to 'pull' the calf out.

The calf was delivered dead. I placed some hay around the heifer to make her comfortable. She hadn't gotten up when I left. I tried to make the best of a bad situation. That was all I could do.

Later, back in the car, my father asked me, "Why did you bother to pull that calf? The heifer hasn't got much of a chance."

"I know," I answered. "I did not do all that work for the client, I did it for the cow. I probably won't get paid, but my job is to help animals."

I heard Dad mutter to himself. "It's all about caring."

To me he said, " I am proud of you."

13

Ellie informed me that I was to be a father again. We knew the Lustron metal house would be too small for two kids, so we started looking for a larger home. We were interested in renting, since I still wasn't sure of the future.

We looked at several houses and settled on a large Victorian house, built in 1912 by rich miners. The house was in poor condition, gloomy inside, with dark, depressing woodwork. Ellie insisted that it was the best house we had seen. She assured me that it would look much better with lighter colored paint on the walls.

I didn't have time to help so Ellie took Debbie and started the process of cleaning and painting. Ellie had just finished painting a cabinet when Debbie, a toddler by now, thought the low shelf, which was just her size, would be a nice place to sit. She got wet paint all over the seat of her pants. The only thing Ellie could do was laugh.

We moved the day President Kennedy was assassinated. Bill Monahan, one of our moving day volunteers, heard the news on the radio and informed the rest of us. We stopped moving for a while, turned on our television set, and followed the news events as they occurred. Everyone was in a state of shock.

"Do you remember what you were doing when the president was shot?" has been a common question. I remember it well.

My client base was increasing, and I was working many hours. To save time, I decided to buy two-way radios for instant communication. I moved the office from downtown to an extra room at the back of the house. Ellie would answer the telephone and take care of our office needs.

I hired Evelyn to answer the phone when Ellie was away from home. Evelyn was given an office extension phone in her home along with a 2-way radio unit. The veterinary office phone was always answered, and I could be reached quickly using the two-way radio.

On February 19, 1964, Steven Michael Landau was born to two happy parents. I was at the hospital during the labor and the birth, but once I was assured mother and baby were doing well, I got back in my car and started making calls.

According to Jewish law, baby boys are circumcised when they are eight days old. The tradition comes from the book of Genesis when Abraham entered into a covenant with God, which required all Jewish males to be circumcised. We needed to find a *mohel*, a Jewish man who is specially trained to perform the surgery. The nearest one I could find was in Minneapolis, MN. I called him, and he said he would be happy to come and help us with the *mitzvah* (obeying a commandant of God). He told me he travels all over the upper Midwest to perform the *Bris* for Jewish parents.

After Ellie and Steve were home for a few days, we had the ceremony. The *mohel* examined Steve very carefully before beginning the surgery. The *mitzvah* is not performed if it would be harmful to the baby.

Our parents came to Shullsburg and brought the food for the party, which was held following the ceremony. Food is a must at a Jewish party. We invited many of our friends to join us for this joyous occasion.

Welcome to the family, Steve.

14

A 3-1/2-acre plot of land was for sale about a block from our rented house. I bought it so we could build our own home.

Shortly after closing on the lot, I came home to find a group of men standing in the yard of the rented house. I asked them what they wanted. They said that they represented a real estate agency, which was going to put our rented house up for sale.

"Are you interested in making a bid?" they asked.

"I own a lot, and will be building a new house," I told them.

They insisted that I make an offer. I thought about it and offered a ridiculously low bid for the house, garage, and summer-kitchen. They chuckled and said, "The owners would never consider such a low price. Thanks anyway." I went back to work, not giving the conversation a second thought.

Two months later the real estate agency called saying the owners of our rented house had accepted my bid. We were now going to be the owners of this large house that we were renting.

Ellie and I didn't know whether to be happy or upset. Now we would be remodeling an old house rather than building a new one. However, we had purchased a very good house at a bargain price and would not be forced to move.

My veterinary practice was expanding. I was working many hours. Evening and night calls were the hardest. During evening chores, farmers often found problems that they felt needed immediate attention. I would go if the client thought that it was a real emergency, and the problem could not wait till morning. After that came late night emergencies such as calving and milkfever.

I hated community events such as football games, because farmers came home late and checked the animals in the barn before going to bed. If they discovered any problems, they would call and wake me. Some nights were so bad that I would work until the sun brightened the eastern sky.

Larry Johnson reminded me of a time when he called late at night and woke me up. I muttered into the phone. "You had better have a good reason for calling at this time of night".

He had an actual emergency. His cow had severe milkfever and would have died if I had not treated her immediately.

On many farm visits, I am faced with the "while you're here, Doc", syndrome. This means the farmer has other cows that need veterinary attention. Sometimes these other cows have symptoms much worse then the initial case. Even the calls in the middle of the night were not immune to this syndrome. Occasionally, the calving calls were less work than the "while you're here, Doc" cases.

Jim Stubes had a middle of the night OB, which was easy, but the cow next to her was suffering an allergic reaction. She was shaking, bellowing, had her tongue hanging out, and developing signs of hives. The white portion of her skin seemed to be swelling and turning red. Huge blisters were forming, and her breathing was becoming difficult. The cow's eyes were wide with panic.

"What's wrong with this cow?" Jim asked in a shaken voice.

Sleep disappeared from my foggy brain. I ran to the car for epinephrine and antihistamines. The epinephrine needed to be injected into the jugular vein to achieve the quickest response.

Somehow, the cow had to be restrained. I grabbed a halter and positioned it on her head. Frantically, I searched for the vein in her neck, jabbed it with a needle and saw dark red coming out. I had hit the vein. I attached the syringe to the needle and pushed in the plunger watching the clear fluid of epinephrine disappear. Now we had to wait.

Slowly the hard breathing began to subside, and the cow appeared less frightened. I gave her antihistamines in the muscle. Jim and I watched her until she was stable.

"What brought that on?" he asked.

"I have no clue," I confessed.

I drove home, fully awake, with no hope of falling back to sleep. I grabbed a veterinary book and started reading. I must have finally dozed off, because I remember being awakened by the ringing of the phone, which was the first call of the morning.

Jim told me later that his cow was fine. The cause of the allergic reaction remains a mystery.

15

Odors are problems for anyone who works with animals. Smells from feces, urine, ammonia gases, rotting flesh, and bacterial infections can nauseate anyone. To the veterinarians, the odors and the smells are so common that we become desensitized, and don't realize that we may smell bad. The stench gets in the car and on clothing. The skin and hair become a collector of these disgusting smells. I was oblivious to the odors, but the moment I walked into the house, Ellie could tell what kind of work I was doing. She has an acute sense of smell.

I tried very hard to eliminate the odors that lingered on me. A good scrub washed away the dirt and decaying tissue but the smell could remain for days. I even protected myself with shoulder length plastic gloves and sleeves but they were only a minimal help. In time, the odor would dissipate, but a new odiferous case would present itself, and I smelled all over again. Masking the odors with after-shave was partially effective.

The odors that lasted the longest were from neglected obstetrical cases where the calf had died and was putrefying inside the uterus. I had to remove the fetus to give the mother a chance of survival. Saving the life of a cow gave me a sense of achievement.

To accomplish an extraction of a dead calf requires complete concentration on the procedure, and full immersion into the offending body fluids. Once the calf was out and the noxious liquids released, the toxin levels would drop, and the cow would show immediate improvement.

Unventilated hog barns are particularly offensive. I never developed a tolerance to that smell. I preferred working on hogs outside, where the odors and dust can be dissipated into the open air.

Sometimes, a sow would have trouble farrowing in the middle of the night. I would have to get out of bed and drive to the hog farm to assist her deliver her piglets. When I returned to a sleeping Ellie, I made sure not to disturb her or she would request I immediately take a shower.

Animal odors are a part of my profession, and I can tolerate them, but human BO is very offensive to me. There isn't any excuse for an unclean body.

New innovations and techniques may someday be developed to mask farm animal odors. For me, they were annoying, embarrassing and unwanted, but they were a 'side effect' of the profession.

16

I had reached my physical limit. I was overworked and not getting enough sleep. I was fighting a cold, but it won. I was hospitalized for three days with pneumonia. I knew I could no longer keep up with my workload. I had started the practice from nothing, but now, I had more work than I could physically handle. I had to choose between leaving Shullsburg and working in a multi-person practice, or hiring someone to work with me.

When I was recouping at home, a man came to the door. He introduced himself as Dr. Al Kramer. He said he was presently working in Orangeville, IL, but that arrangement was becoming uncertain. He was driving around the area looking for a place to start his own veterinary practice.

I told him he had come to the right place. The Shullsburg area had enough work for more than one veterinarian. I suggested that he consider establishing his own practice here in Shullsburg, or work with me.

He seemed interested in working with me, but before he could make a commitment, he had to consult with his wife, Marsha. Several days later, the Kramer family drove to Shullsburg to discuss the job offer. We made an agreement, and Al started working for me. The Kramers had three children, about the same age as ours, and the families were very compatible.

What intrigued me most about Al was his intellect and memory. Extremely intelligent people are never satisfied and constantly search for new ideas and experiences. It was hard for me to keep up with him, but it was fun to try. The harder I was challenged, the more I would respond. Together we were a great team. He made me a better veterinarian. In six months, he became an equal partner, and we formed Shullsburg Veterinary Service.

Shullsburg Veterinary Service needed more office space than the one room in my house. Dr. Whitehall had passed away. His widow still lived in the apartment above his office, and she wanted to sell the building and move away. It would be an ideal office for SVS.

Al and I agreed to buy the building from Mrs. Whitehall. SVS would have its own domain. Ellie was overjoyed. She would be relieved of the responsibility of answering the phone and contacting us on the two-way radio. The farmers would be going to the office to pick up medications rather than coming to our house at any time of day or night.

Our next job was to find a secretary to do the jobs that Ellie and Marsha had done. We wanted the business to grow and needed a dependable person with a good personality who had some farm background. Al said he knew a woman who had these qualifications. Adda Kittoe agreed to become our secretary.

Adda, the mother of six children, was extremely honest, intelligent, and dependable. She had the perfect personality for our business, had been the wife of a farmer, and could sympathize with the problems of our clients. We had found the perfect person to take care of our new office.

The team of Adda, Al and Louie became very successful. Al and I kept ourselves informed by attending meetings and classes, reading about new developments in farm animal practice, and challenging each other to do better. Our goal was to develop the best and most modern practice in our area.

17

Cows are high maintenance creatures that need constant care and attention, much like babies. A dairy cow needs to be milked at least two times a day. Feed needs to be available 24 hours a day. Excellent management determines the financial success of the farm.

Veterinary assistance is a contributing factor to the reproductive efficiency in a client's herd. Maintaining reproduction is a formidable task that often influences the economic outcome of farm owners, landlords, and families. Reproductive failures could cause some family farms to go into financial ruin.

The gestation period for cows is nine months. A cow should have a calf every 12-14 months. During the remaining 3-5 months, the animal must have excellent care in order to be healthy and ready to conceive again.

A record is required for each cow in a herd. Relying on memory is not sufficient for keeping track of the required information that is necessary for maintaining good reproductive performance.

I became a bovine gynecologist. I dictated the pertinent details that should be entered on each cows' health record. Fertility exams are done rectally and are quite accurate. My examination on each cow started 30 days after calving. If I detected a problem, I administered drugs and treatments. I suggested a recheck date that was entered on her record. If the cow was normal and showed heat, 'to be bred' and 'check for pregnancy' would be entered on her record.

Stan Cox, a progressive dairyman, who was trying to improve his herd of cows, realized I was still a novice at detecting the first signs of pregnancy. "You'll have to do better then this," he said when I started doing fertility exams for his herd. "You can't just guess. You have to determine pregnancies as early as 35 days. If you can't do better than that I'll have to call another veterinarian."

"I'll be ready next month," I said. That day, I started studying theriogenology, the study of reproduction, and it became part of my life. I developed programs and drug regimens with the goal of getting cows to conceive on a timely basis and live a long and productive life.

Accurate rectal exams were the essence of this approach. Examining cows for reproductive problems and determining pregnancy was accomplished by feeling the reproductive organs through the rectum.

I had read that sterile monkeys were responding to steroid medication and becoming pregnant. Steroids are closely related to sex hormones, so I theorized that somehow an additional hormone-like treatment might stimulate cows to get pregnant. I called my concoction MJ, for monkey juice. It seemed to work. MJ was a popular treatment, and new clients were calling me to assist with their cows that were having fertility problems.

A few years later, the actual hormones were being manufactured and were more effective. They replaced MJ, but for a while, my untested therapy was a hit.

The initial fertility programs expanded into monthly herd checks. Each morning, I visited the dairy farm that had a standing appointment for that day. My calendar for the month revolved around these appointments.

I realized the additional information that I acquired during the herd checks could go beyond fertility evaluations. Nutritional recommendations could be made, cow comfort could be discussed, and sick cows could be treated early. When I did the rectal examination, I could identify a fever by the heat generated against my hand and arm. New clients wanted these services, and I tried to accommodate all of them.

18

Thanksgiving, 1966, had come and gone. Now the days were filled with anticipation. Our family was waiting for the arrival of our third baby. In preparation for the additional family member, we had purchased a new car, a large white Dodge 880, 4-door sedan, with a huge engine. I needed a dependable car to take Ellie to the hospital.

We also had purchased a new luxurious king-sized bed for extra comfort. I thoroughly enjoyed sleeping on that extra large mattress. My feet did not hang off the end of the bed.

Early Christmas morning Ellie woke me. She was in labor. "Big deal", I thought. She was in labor for a long time delivering the other two children. The contorted look on her face, and her muffled cries assured me this delivery would be different. The contractions were very close together, and I had to get her to the hospital quickly. I can deliver a calf, but I certainly did not want to deliver my own child.

We had arranged to have my Mom and Dad come to Shullsburg and stay with Debbie and Steve. I called them and attempted to coherently tell them to get here as soon as possible. Somehow, I quickly got dressed and ran out to the garage to get the car and bring it around to the front of the house. I left the car running to warm it up and ran into the house. As I entered the house I heard the cry, "It's coming, it's coming!"

I grabbed the phone to call Clara Probst our neighbor. She had seen me running around the house, and knew something was up. I told her we had to get to the hospital **NOW**, and I asked her if she would she watch Debbie and Steve until my parents could get to Shullsburg. I ran back upstairs to help Ellie.

She was still in bed! "I can't get up. It hurts too much," she sobbed.

"You can't have that baby on the new bed," I told her. I did not want to have to deliver that baby!

My insensitivity infuriated Ellie so much that she got out of bed, struggled into some clothing, and waddled painfully down the stairs and out to the car.

Clara had ran across the street with a coat over her nightgown and was comforting Debbie and Steve. I heard Debbie say, "Mom, you forgot to put on lipstick". The kids always knew we were going somewhere when Ellie put on lipstick.

The hospital was 12 miles away in Cuba City. I got to the highway, and since it was Christmas morning, there was no one on the road. I was driving 80 mph with Ellie yelling; "It's coming!"

"Cross your legs," was my response, but it was definitely not appreciated.

I whizzed through Benton wanting a police escort, but the place was like a ghost town. I did not see anyone. I had five more miles to go. The contractions had eased momentarily, so Ellie was a little more comfortable. I squealed the car to a stop in front of the emergency room door of the hospital. I dashed in shouting, "My wife is having a baby in the car".

A nurse rushed out with a wheel chair. Ellie slowly eased herself out of the car and into the wheel chair, and we headed directly to the delivery room.

Dr. King was making his rounds. Ellie's look conveyed the message that the baby was coming. He took off his sport coat and followed the nurse pushing Ellie into the delivery room.

David Scott Landau was born 12 minutes after our arrival at the Cuba City Hospital. David was normal in every way. Ellie forgave me for my insensitive comments.

While Ellie and David were in the hospital, a severe snowstorm lashed southwestern Wisconsin. All schools were closed. The morning shift of the hospital staff could not get to work, so the night staff had to stay and work an extra shift.

Undaunted, I braved the storm to visit a surprised Ellie. Ellie thought the visit was to prove to everyone that weather would not stop me, and it was the male thing to do. Maybe she was right.

After five days, the normal hospital stay for delivering a baby, David and Ellie came home. My parents greeted us at the door with packed suitcases. They kissed the baby, kissed Ellie and left for their home near Scioto Mills, Illinois. They needed to check for storm damage at their farm.

Debbie and Steve had just awakened from their nap. I was way behind on my calls, and had to leave. Ellie was left alone to care for the two small kids and the new baby. I don't know how she did it.

Debbie came through to lighten the tension. Upon seeing her new brother, she said, "Mom, we got another boy because you were not wearing lipstick when you went to the hospital. If you had looked nice, maybe a girl would have come instead".

We had a *Bris* much like Steve's, with a party, food and friends. Wow, three kids, a wonderful wife, and more joy then I could imagine.

Welcome to the family, David.

19

There had been a lot of rain in the Shullsburg area that spring. The grass was tall flourishing in the ideal weather for optimum growth. Rain clouds were again looming in the western sky. There would be more rain soon.

Bob Olson had called the office with an urgent plea. "Doc, come quick! My cows are acting weird." I had a bad feeling about this call. With great trepidation, I drove to Bob's farm to try to determine the problem with his cows.

Bob met me at the entrance of his barn. His expression indicated deep concern and worry. Bob is an excellent farmer and dairyman, and the look on his face frightened me. He normally was happy and unconcerned, but not this time.

We walked to the yard where his cows had gathered for the night milking, and I became as concerned as Bob. Many cows were staggering, some were trembling, and others were going into convulsions. All his cows were affected.

"Do something," Bob pleaded.

I didn't know what was causing the problem with the cows. My mind was racing with possibilities. A disease needed an incubation period. Not all animals would be affected the same or at the same time. Some of the cows would be able to suppress an infection with their immune system.

Bob was current on his vaccination schedule. He and his family were good managers. This herd of cows produced a lot of milk. No unusual problems had been observed at morning milking.

What had changed during the day? We checked with his sons, and no one could give me an answer. They assured me everything was the same.

"When was the last time you ground new feed?" I asked in desperation. "This morning after milking," one of the boys replied. The cows were eating this batch of feed for the first time.

Then I heard someone gasp. He remembered that a bag of insecticide had been stored in the feed room. It must have been added to the grain mix instead of salt. The cows were suffering from Aldrin poisoning.

The bag of the insecticide lists the drugs that can be used as an antidote for its contents. A barbiturate or anesthetic was the drug of choice to counteract the Aldrin. We needed to anesthetize all the cows that were showing signs of poisoning.

I called Al to come and help and to bring along all the general anesthetic that was in the office. I started intravenous treatment with the anesthetic I had in my truck.

We did not have enough barbiturate in our inventory to treat all the animals. We sent people to every veterinary clinic in our area. Everyone responded to the emergency by allowing us to take all the anesthetics they could spare. There still wasn't enough to help all the cows.

We phoned a pharmaceutical distributor in Madison, WI, 75 miles away. The company manager went to the warehouse and loaded his car with all the anesthetics they had. Since time was crucial, he personally delivered the drugs to our office.

Administering anesthetics to cows is challenging. Their eructation mechanism, responsible for cows being able to chew their cuds, can be paralyzed. Stomach contents can get into the nose and be inhaled into the lung causing foreign body pneumonia that leads to a slow and agonizing death in cows. We needed to maintain a level of anesthesia but we did not want to paralyze the swallowing reflex.

The barn floor was covered with comatose cows. The entire area was black and white, the color of Holsteins. There was barely enough room to move.

A certain level of anesthesia had to be maintained to prevent convulsions. If a cow would start convulsing, she would be given more anesthetic.

My partner monitored the herd during the night, and I relieved him in the morning. The around-the-clock watch went on for three days. Finally, cows were waking up with no symptoms. We and the cows had survived the crisis.

In the rain, Bob and his family went to the pasture with flashlights, looking for cows missing from the barn. They were able to find all but three. The tall grass and rain hid them. All the ones treated lived, and those not found died.

There was another price that no one had anticipated. Aldrin is a fat-soluble toxin, making milk and meat inedible for human consumption. Activated charcoal is a detoxifier. It absorbs toxin when released from fat.

It took nine months and thousands of dollars worth of activated charcoal before the toxin declined to safe levels, and the meat and milk could be sold.

Dumped milk caused the farm to smell sour, and the inside of the barn turned black due to all the charcoal that was fed to the cows. Yet, Bob and his family survived. It was a terrible financial drain, but they still milk cows, and the disaster is a bad memory and a worse dream.

20

The 60's were filled with the Landau family expansion and building a practice. In the fall of 1967, Ellie became pregnant again. I was looking forward to a new baby. Of course I would. I didn't have to carry the baby and put up with all the extra work. After all, I just needed to "make a living."

Al and I had a good partnership, and we were making money. It was an exciting time for all of us.

The practice decided to lease four-wheel drive trucks and buy veterinary medical units that attached to the chassis of the trucks. The units were designed to carry veterinary instruments, equipment, and drugs. There were water tanks that supplied hot and cold running water.

A truck is easier for me to drive, and the seats were more comfortable. My back had been hurting causing me to walk unnaturally.

Al ordered his truck first. We were impressed. The truck part was leased in Shullsburg; the medical body was manufactured in Iowa. Al drove his truck to the middle of Iowa to have the medical unit installed on the chassis.

When my truck arrived, I asked Dad to accompany me to Iowa. It would be an overnight trip and a bouncy ride in the boxless truck. Even though he knew he had to endure these discomforts, Dad was delighted to accompany me.

I was a little concerned when I noticed that Dad wasn't as mobile as he had been. He struggled to climb stairs and tired easily. I attributed these problems to his being overweight and out of shape. He had suffered a heart attack some years earlier, but had not experienced any problems recently. We talked all the way there and back. We thoroughly enjoyed being with each other.

21

Traumatic reticulitis is the medical term that describes hardware in ruminants. A foreign object penetrates the reticulum or second stomach and causes an infection. The treatment for this problem is usually a magnet, some digestive boluses, and antibiotics. Most cows recover without side effects. Some dairymen think veterinarians make the diagnosis too often, and use it as a 'catch all'. Some think it is used to cover up another problem that may be overlooked. Perhaps, that's true, but hardware or traumatic reticulitis displays a group of symptoms that are hard to ignore.

A slight fever is symptomatic of hardware. 'Normal' bovine rectal temperature is between 101° and 102°. Hardware creates a small increase that registers about 103° to 104°. This temperature is caused by the infection at the site of penetration. Low-grade fever is typical of peritonitis or infection of the peritoneum, the inside lining covering of the abdomen.

Higher heart rate may also be a symptom of hardware. The reticulum is located next to the diaphragm and close to the heart. Pressure here causes the heart to work harder. The foreign body may pierce the reticulum, go through the diaphragm, and end up in the heart. Sacks around the heart may fill with pus creating pericarditis. If a sloshing sound replaces heart sounds, the animal is close to death due to pericarditis.

Enlarged jugular veins are still another possible symptom of hardware. Since the heart is stressed and overworked, blood will not be pumped fast enough, and the jugular veins will enlarge in the neck. A jugular pulse may be seen. Fluids may collect under the jaw due to cardiac insufficiency. Most animals are treated before traumatic reticulitis gets this advanced.

Pain is another possible symptom of hardware. Animals suffering from hardware arch their backs and stand hunched. A diagnostician, pressing on the sternum of an animal, may cause the cow to grunt due to pain.

Many cows are treated for hardware by administering magnets. If the penetrating objects are metal and can be attracted to the magnet, the foreign material is pulled back and the wound heals.

Magnets are about three inches long and can be round or rectangular. A grooved magnet was recently invented, which provides a larger area of attachment.

Magnets have two poles, one positive and one negative. If an animal has been treated for hardware in the past, that magnet may still be in the reticulum. If another one is inserted, the positive pole on one of the magnets will attract the negative pole on the other and neither magnet will be effective in attracting foreign metal. Newer magnets, which consist of smaller magnetized pieces of magnet held together by plastic, may prevent the canceling effect.

"Want to buy some magnets?" Jerry asked. "Selling them real cheap." With that, Jerry held out a plastic bucket that had about a hundred magnets of varying size and description.

"Where did you get them?" I asked, guessing the answer. Jerry worked at the local slaughter plant and retrieved the magnets from the kill floor.

"I can't tell you," he said mysteriously. I would have bet that some of those were ones I had put into animals I had diagnosed with hardware.

"I can't use them because they are old and have lost some magnetism," I said.

"Your loss Doc," Jerry said as he walked out the door.

Magnets are fragile and when dropped or used may become less powerful. I checked every magnet I used by placing it on the truck and pulling it off. If it had lost magnetism, it either would have slid down the metal surface or offer little resistance to removal. I did not want to use faulty magnets.

Randy Madison had three cows he thought were sick. All were off-feed and down on milk. Randy was a good manager and was concerned about his animals.

"Got to get these cows back on-feed," Randy said. My examination revealed that all the cows had slightly elevated temperatures and no rumen movements. They liked standing with their back feet in the gutters, which I interpreted to be pain. Heart rates were slightly increased.

"I think all three cows have hardware," I told Randy.

"I have had a single cow with hardware but never three at the same time... You're sure?" Randy asked.

"It's hard to diagnose hardware, Randy," I said. "I want to see the feed bunk."

We walked outside and inspected the feed. Most of the silage had been eaten, but there were many pieces of chopped-up fence wire that were 2 or 3 inches long. The wire had sharp ends that could penetrate the stomach.

"Guess you found the source," Randy said in amazement. "Now what should I do?"

"Start by removing this picked over silage that contains the metal. Then run silage from the silo until you get past the wire," I said.

"Next, I will treat the sick cows. I will leave magnets with you and a stainless steal balling gun to use so that you can make the cows swallow the magnets." Magnets do not stick to stainless steel.

"Can I give magnets to cows that aren't sick?" Randy wanted to know.

"Sure, they won't hurt anything," I answered. Because of their weight and size magnets go directly to the reticulum where they are suppose to stay. The reticulum has an inside lining that appears like a honeycomb. When sharp foreign objects get caught in the honeycomb, they can penetrate it and cause traumatic reticulitis. Magnets may keep these objects away from the wall by holding on to the metal. Even cows without symptoms may benefit from magnets.

"Could something like plastic cause hardware?" Randy asked.

"Of course," I said. "If that happens, we need to perform surgery called a rumenotomy. We enter the rumen on the left side and feel around with our hand for a foreign object in the reticulum. Hopefully the object is found and removed."

Randy's cows did not need surgery. They started eating again and production improved. Two more cows became sick from the adulterated silage. Randy treated them with magnets and antibiotics. They improved and luckily, the incident did not create lasting problems.

Once inserted, magnets may not necessarily remain in the reticulum. Some can be vomited and others are passed through the rest of the digestive tract.

Once, I was doing surgery to correct a twisted stomach and felt a hard object in the small intestine. It was loose, and I could move it. I made a small incision in the intestine and worked the object out. It was a magnet that had left the reticulum and was traveling through the digestive tract.

Hardware is a prevalent problem. Construction, machine failures, and carelessness are the primary source of foreign objects that get into cows. Roofing nails are a common cause of penetration. Old buildings are an abundant source of nails.

Frequently, in a new construction area, nails are dropped. Areas around new buildings should be cleaned up before any cattle are allowed in them. Magnets may be given to prevent traumatic reticulitis.

22

There was a client who just loved to give me verbal abuse. He owned a large herd of 80 milk cows. We had wonderful word exchanges that became a part of my visits to treat sick cows. His large family actively helped in the barn and took the responsibility of managing his large herd of cows. Greg Ellis, one of the older sons seemed to be the boss.

On a routine visit to the farm, I observed Greg's father, Phil, attempting to go from a tractor to another piece of equipment. He was stumbling and tripping. He was having a very difficult time walking.

In keeping with our usual banter, I yelled out some obscene remark about his consumption of alcohol. Greg heard the comment and immediately came over to talk to me. I commented to Greg about his father "hitting the bottle".

"My father isn't drunk," Greg said. "He has multiple sclerosis."

Greg advised me to say nothing to his father about the illness. "Keep up your normal banter," he suggested, which I tried to do, but the fun was gone.

Several days after this encounter, I was scheduled to attend a meeting in San Antonio, Texas. Part of the agenda was devoted to a possible cure for MS. Perhaps I could learn something to help Phil. I signed up for the classes.

The theory stated that MS and dog distemper were the same virus. Inoculate non-lactating udders of cows with the dog vaccine, and the cows will produce antibodies that humans can use. When the cows have their calves, the colostrum, rich in antibodies, will help human patients.

When I returned home, I went to see Greg. I related the information I had received, and Greg said he would tell his dad. Phil was excited with the prospect of something that might work.

We inoculated three of the best cows in the herd. There was more than enough colostrum produced. The only beneficial effect was that Phil received from the colostrum was to gain weight. He had been extremely thin.

His disease did not improve, and he died about a year later. Now we know that this whole approach was futile. Modern medicine is still working on the cause and cure of MS. Some new medications have been proven to help, but they were not developed in time to help Phil.

23

Winter isn't always fun in Wisconsin. A winter wonderland may exist in books and pictures but living and working in winter weather can be extremely challenging.

The snow and strong wind of a winter storm can cut visibility to zero, and blind a driver no matter how well the vehicle is equipped. If the air temperature climbs above freezing, the water in the air condenses over the snow causing fog so dense that light penetration is impossible. Freezing rain creates glazed ice on the roads allowing vehicles to slide in any direction regardless of the attempt of the driver to control its movement.

On icy road conditions a vehicle without four-wheel drive, can be trapped between two hills. It is too slippery to drive up the hill facing the vehicle, and nearly impossible to back up the hill that is behind the vehicle. There is always the risk of sliding off the road into a ditch.

Ellie and I found ourselves on glare ice driving home one winter night. I had driven into Dubuque to meet her after work and see a play. We were each driving a car on our way home. There had been a weather forecast for freezing rain later that night, but it arrived earlier than expected. About two miles from Dubuque, we started to drive through a light rain. As we continued easterly, the rain changed to sleet and then ice. Oh, I wish we had stayed in Dubuque.

We had slowly crept along about 20 miles, with

10 miles remaining, when we had to climb a hill on the west side of Benton. I was able to coax my car up that hill, but I saw the lights of Ellie's car on the apron of the road and knew she was sliding and not getting anywhere.

I parked my car and attempted to walk back to her. The road was totally covered with ice. Somehow I got there by slipping, sliding and stumbling.

"What are we going to do now?" Ellie asked me.

"Move over. I will drive this car up that hill so we can get to Benton," I replied.

"How are you going to do that?" she asked.

"I don't know," I growled, as the ice kept building on the windshield. The wipers had no chance of keeping up with this freezing rain.

As I leaned out the driver's door to see where I was going, I backed the car up the opposing hill as far as the ice would let me. Then, I began driving forward trying go as fast as possible and yet being cautious at the same time. I only got a little more than half way up the hill.

"Now what?" my wife asked.

"I'll try again," I said. I think she would have gotten out if she could.

I was more determined then ever. I kept trying until I finally made it to the top of that hill. It was a small accomplishment. We were still out in the country, ten miles from home.

"You have to drive this car to Benton," I stated.

"No way," was her response.

Benton was 1-1/2 miles away on a gently rolling roadway with the ditches on both sides of the road.

I know she was scared, but we couldn't just leave the car out there on top of a hill out in the country. Someone else might slide into it.

If she would drive it into Benton, I promised her we would park it there, and I would drive the rest of the way home. We drove very slowly and made it into Benton without any further problems.

We parked her car under a street light on a level stretch of road on the deserted street. We were eight miles from our front door.

We started for Shullsburg. At least, we were together. It had stopped raining, and the layer of ice wasn't getting any thicker.

The road goes downhill east of Benton before starting uphill again. I was feeling pretty confident, until my headlights illuminated the area. About ten cars were lining both sides of the road, some in the ditches and some on the shoulder.

I was able to get past most of them and almost made it to the top. Then I, too, could not coax my car to go forward any farther and rolled back to the bottom of the hill.

We sat with the other stranded motorists on the side of the road, for a short time. Then, I turned around and went back into Benton hoping to think of a way to get home. I really did not want to spend the night in the car.

After a half an hour, we heard a siren screaming its warning somewhere in the distance. The sound was coming from the east. I watched in amazement as the red light pierced the darkness.

"How was it able to travel on this ice?" I thought. As the Shullsburg ambulance rushed past, hurrying someone to the hospital, I heard the clinking sound of its tire chains.

Quickly, I started the car and drove east on the wrong side of the road following the path made by the ambulance. The chains had scarred the ice, and now there was enough traction for my car to get up the hill on the east side of Benton. There were more hills to conquer before we could get home, but we finally made it.

My truck is better equipped for Wisconsin winter weather. It is higher off the ground for better visibility, and it has four-wheel drive. It also has the two-way radio communication, so I can call for help if necessary.

A howling wind was blowing from the north adding additional chill to the minus 20° F temperature on an early winter morning, when I was responding to an emergency call. The wind was whipping the new snow that was mixing with the snow already on the ground. Visibility was zero. No one had left tracks in the snow on the small gravel road I was traveling. A wrong nudge of the steering wheel would be disastrous, because my truck and I would end up in a ditch.

The only light available was coming from my headlights, as they were attempting to penetrate the mesmerizing snow. I had turned off the lights on the instrument panel hoping for better visibility as I was driving through the whiteout. I had engaged the four-wheel drive mechanism to ensure the best possible traction available, but my tires were losing their grip.

"Hold on, I'll be there shortly," I kept telling myself. "The barn should appear soon." Since all the landmarks were obliterated by the blowing snow, I wasn't quite sure of my exact location.

Vic Schultz had phoned an hour earlier. He had gotten up to check his cow that was ready to calve and called me immediately when he discovered that the new mother was not able to get up.

Finally, the farm's yard light came into view. As I turned the truck to enter the farmyard, I hoped I was on the driveway and not heading into the ditch. So far, so good. My object was to get as close to the barn as possible. I didn't want to be out in the weather any longer than necessary. I cautiously opened the truck door. It was almost wrenched from my hand by the wind.

My arrival was met with much relief. "Am I ever glad to see you," Vic said. I gathered my supplies and equipment and followed Vic as he led the way through the deep snow to the barn.

The barn was cozy and warm, quite a contrast to the frigid temperatures outside. I glanced down the two rows of contented animals. Most of the 70 cows were lying down, munching hay. They didn't seem concerned that a raging storm was blowing outside, or that a stranger had entered the barn.

The cow had given birth in the middle of the night and now was unconscious with milkfever. A red, swollen and enlarged prolapsed uterus protruded from her vulva. After the calf was born, the cow continued straining and the uterus was turned inside-out.

The calf was still wet. It was alive and seemed ok, but it needed its mother's milk to survive.

"Can you save the cow?" Vic asked pleadingly. "She looks like she is dying". I agreed with Vic. The cow's breathing was shallow, and her eyes dry and unmoving. Vic paced back and forth not really knowing what to do or what to say. I wasn't very encouraged with the animal's chance for survival, but I had to try.

I started by finding the jugular vein in the neck of the cow and began the process of administering the life-saving fluids. Slowly, the new mother began to respond. Her eyes began to tear and were losing the dryness, that I had observed before starting the treatment. She began to awaken from her deep and deadly sleep.

"She might make it, don't you think, Doc?" asked Vic, very worried and still pacing back and forth along the front of the pen.

"She has a chance," was all I could offer. Some cows did not survive beyond this stage. They would have a heart attack and then die. This patient was becoming alert, which boosted my confidence. Soon she sat up and began looking for her calf.

The treatment for the milkfever was successful, but now I had to deal with the prolapsed uterus.

Vic and I needed our combined strength to lift and fold the uterus back through the vagina. Finally, we were able to replace it. The cow got up to lick her calf and let it nurse. "I think she'll be all right," I managed to say as my muscles began to relax.

"Thank you, Doc, for coming out in a night like this to save my cow." The fury of the wind could still be heard through the barn walls, but I felt contented, with the successful ending to a difficult situation.

I washed all the instruments and tried to remove most of the grime and dirt from my insulated coveralls. Vic helped me carry all my supplies and tools back to my truck.

The night sky was giving way to daylight as I started the engine. I picked up the microphone on the two-way radio to report that I had finished with this job and was coming home.

To my surprise, Ellie said two more emergencies had come in. The storm and wind continued as I wondered what new adventures were waiting. It was the start of another day.

Winter gives way to spring and a rejuvenation of life, but this spring would be quite different for me.

24

Dad suffered a heart attack in the spring of 1968. He was put in intensive care, but was able to talk. He told me once again he was very proud of me. He smiled when I told him about his grandchildren and his pregnant daughter-in-law. "She is giving me such a hard time," I complained.

He seemed to enjoy my stories of mistreatment at the hands of Ellie, who was in a fowl mood fighting the discomfort associated with pregnancy. I watched Dad's heart monitor and noted that his EKG was far from normal. I was sure that this was a temporary setback, and our talk was part of his recovery. I had made him laugh.

Mom had been exhausted and had gone home earlier in the evening. I left the hospital buoyed with my conversation with Dad. I even stopped for an ice cream cone. When I got home, I told Ellie that I thought Dad would make it.

I received the call about 2:00 a.m. on May 11 that Dad had died in his sleep. I told the person calling, that I would notify my mother.

I got dressed and got into the car for the 45-mile drive to my parents' farm. As I drove, thoughts of the past entered my mind. Tears streamed down my face, often blurring my vision.

I pulled into the driveway of the farm about 3:00 a.m. The place was dark except for the yard light. I knew Mom would be was sound asleep, and I would have a hard time waking her.

I could have let myself in the house using my key, but I felt waking her with a touch would have badly frightened her. I knocked on the door, and I honked the horn of my car. I finally was able to arouse her by tapping on the window by the bed.

When she realized it was me, she got out of bed and walked through the house to unlocked the door. I didn't have to say anything. She immediately knew the reason of my middle of the night visit. We cried, holding on to each other. We talked about the past and the future.

I phoned Jenny and Paul DeVidal, my parents' best friends, who lived in Freeport, IL. In order to give comfort and support to my mother, they arrived at the farm before daylight. Paul, Jenny, Mom and I were sat at the kitchen table thinking and speaking of how my father had influenced our lives.

The mood changed when Ellie and our three children arrived at 8 a.m. The kids ran in yelling "Grammy Paula" and hugged her. A twinkle appeared in her eyes along with some tears. Grammy was needed, and some of the old resolve and strength returned. Ellie held me in her arms making me realize how much she meant to me.

While I was making arrangements for Dad's funeral, I kept thinking of him, and of the many things he had done for me.

Dad was buried in the Jewish cemetery in Rockford Illinois. It was a large funeral. Some of the people who attended were cattle buyers like Dad, others were people who had also been displaced by World War II. The war had changed so many lives.

My mother needed to find her niche without Dad. When he had been sick, she devoted all her time to taking care of him. Now she was alone.

After a few months, Mom applied for a part-time job at a factory in Freeport. She made new friends, and was independent once again. Her resolve and determination gave her a new life. My anxiety about her future was unfounded.

Dad is missed. He left a legacy of hard work, loyalty, and love. Somewhere he is still saying how proud he is of his son. I hope I earned the praise.

We had lost Dad, but a new life in our family was about to be born. Ellie was 8 months pregnant at Dad's funeral. Mom came to stay with us for a while when Ellie went to the hospital.

On June 10, 1968, Judy Ann Landau was born. She wasn't in any hurry to get here. Ellie was in labor for two days. Debbie, who was almost six years old, was very happy to have a sister.

Welcome to the family, Judy.

25

Three fatty acids acetic, proprionic, and butric, are produced by rumen digestion. The way animals are fed determines which of these acids predominate. Dairy cows are fed roughage so more acetic acid is produced. This type of ration produces higher butter fat and more proteins in milk. Feeder cattle are given a grain diet so more proprionic acid predominates. Proprionic acid stimulates production of muscle and body fat.

Bacteria that digest feeds are responsible for fatty acid production. But, it takes time for the bacteria to adjust to changes in rations. For this reason, feed changes need to be done slowly and carefully. Not only should there be concern about which of the fatty acids need to predominate, but buffering the acids is important.

Saliva contains bicarbonate for buffering. Gallons of saliva are swallowed daily. If changes in feed occur too rapidly, it causes indigestion and cud chewing is reduced slowing saliva production needed for buffering.

If not enough saliva is swallowed, acidosis results. Foot problems, declining milk production, twisted stomachs, and even death may result from acidosis. Each time a new ration is formulated, it should be phased in slowly to avoid acidosis.

It may seem odd, but acidosis may lead to foot problems as illustrated in Paul Silver's herd. Paul phoned to complain about a bunch of lame cows.

"Paul, I don't like trimming feet," I said to him trying to avoid the back breaking work of removing excess hoof growth. There are hoof trimmers who come to the farm to do that. They are better equipped than we are."

"I know," he said. "John is scheduled to come in a couple of days."

"Why do you need me?" I asked.

"To help me find out why I have so many lame cows," he said.

I examined his cows and noted the excess hoof growth that concerned Paul. John would remove the excess growth, which would make the cows more comfortable.

"Why do these cows grow so much hoof?" Paul asked.

"Excess hoof growth is usually caused by acidosis," I said, "which is caused by an unbalance of the fatty acids produced by bacterial digestion in the cows. A small unbalance in fatty acids causes low grade acidosis. Acidosis produces toxins that cause artery dilation and more blood goes to the lower extremities. This gives the hoof cells more nutrients, and they reproduce faster," I explained.

"A lot of bad things happen when excess hoof starts to grow. The bone in the hoof rotates, and then the big tendons in the back of the leg are stretched," I added.

"Wow," said Paul. "All this from acidosis. What can I do to help my cows?" Paul asked.

"Long cut roughage help with bacterial digestion and keeps the fatty acids in balance," I responded.

"Yeah," he said, 'but I got steers that only get grain, and they seem all right".

"That's because they are young and will be sold before they founder. Milk cows get to be a lot older," I answered.

"So what do you suggest," Paul asked.

After seeing Paul's ration, I suggested, "Get a nutritionist who will balance the ration. A balanced ration will control fatty acid production. The addition of long stemmed hay and roughage should help."

Paul followed my advice, and although feet problems continued, they were more manageable and less wide widespread.

Paul had chronic acidosis, but acidosis can also be acute. It occurs quickly and can kill.

When Tony Valenti became excited, he would yell.

"Two of my cows had somehow lifted the lid of my ground corn bin and eaten all they could," Tony shouted over the phone. "Is there anyway to save them."

Tony was a little man with a booming voice. He always wore a dirty Brewer cap that hid his eyes so the only way to know how excited he was by how loud he spoke. Tony was very upset. Two of his cows were in tough shape. One was down, and the other was wobbling. Both had extended bellies that 'sloshed' when they moved. The one that couldn't get up was nodding her head and kept her eyes closed. She was near death. The other would soon follow.

Gorging on ground corn can cause acute acidosis, which poisons an animal. E coli organisms, which produce toxins are always in the digestive system. They are controlled by normal digestion. The sudden intake of all that grain killed normal bacteria. Harmful bacteria multiply producing toxins that breakdown the permeability of gut tissue allowing absorption of the toxins into the blood. Body fluids are absorbed into the gut causing dehydration. E coli is always the culprit.

I pumped a mixture of magnesium oxide and activated charcoal into each cow. Magnesium oxide is used to help neutralize acid. Activated charcoal can absorb toxin. I used intravenous fluids to fight dehydration.

"Cows are going to die aren't they, Doc?" Tony yelled.

"I don't know," I answered.

"Sure they are," Tony screamed.

"Give them time," I said.

The next day, the one that was down, had died. The one that was wobbly seemed improved, but stiff. The stiffness was due to acute founder caused by the acidosis. So much blood had entered her feet that layers of horn tissue had separated from the live tissue that produces it.

"Tony, can you stand this cow in cold water or run a hose of cold water on her feet?" I asked.

"Sure," Tony said in a normal voice. "Why you want me to do that?" he asked.

"Cold will constrict arteries and open veins removing blood and the pressure on the hoof layers," I said. "It will help stop some of the pain. I'll give her steroids and antihistamines as well, to help reduce the swelling." I said. "Antibiotics are important to stop infections while the body recovers," I added.

Tony was good in following instructions, and the cow survived. Acidosis stops rumen motility and causes peristalsis to decrease. The abomasums, which is the fourth stomach fills with gas and acts like a balloon. It floats and pushes through the space between the first and second stomachs, resulting in a displaced abomasums or DA.

Jimmy Banfield had too many DA's. Most of his cows had surgery scars on their sides, and milk production was down. "I can't afford to operate like this," he confessed.

"You have to buy hay to fight acidosis," I said.

"I don't want to spend the money," he said.

"Pay me, or buy hay and have more milk," I said.

"You're right," he said but I had heard this before. Jimmy had said he would buy hay each time we had done surgery. This time, he seemed more determined.

Jimmy didn't call for over a month. I must have been too persistent on my demand to buy hay. He was listening to my advice, but perhaps didn't want to follow it.

Jimmy finally called with a calving problem. "How are things going?" I ask hesitantly.

"Great," Jimmy replied. "Milk production is up, and it is paying for all the hay I am buying. Just sorry I hadn't followed your advice a lot earlier," he commented slapping me on the back appreciatively.

26

My lower back usually hurt after a busy day of farm visits. I didn't think the pain was unusual. I felt that I was in good shape. The physical stress of hard work was tiring. Some of the animals I had to wrestle weighed 6 or 7 times more than me.

One bright summer day, in 1971, my children and I were enjoying a few minutes of play. We were tossing a ball around, laughing, yelling, and having a wonderful time. I felt a sudden severe stab of pain in my back. It was so intense that I needed to lie down. I headed back toward the house.

The children followed me, assuming I was just leading them to another place to continue the fun. They were starting to climb all over me as they did every evening, but this pain was overwhelming, and I told the kids they had to leave me alone for a while. They were very disappointed and ran to their mother asking, "What's wrong with Daddy?"

Ellie came over to check out the situation. She looked at me and asked, "What's going on."

I told her I had a severe pain in my back. She gave me a couple aspirins, and I went upstairs and crawled into bed. In bed, I could tolerate the pain, and I fell asleep.

The next morning, I woke up feeling refreshed and ready to go work. I made it to the bottom of the stairs before collapsing with new pain. This time, I could not get up off the floor.

Ellie called our family physician, Dr. King. He said to call an ambulance to take me to the Cuba City hospital.

Once at the hospital, x-rays were taken to help discover the cause of my pain. The x-rays did not show any broken bones. I was put in traction with weights suspended from my legs. The traction released the pressure on my spinal cord. I was given morphine to relieve the excruciating pain.

The stretching of my back was successful, and the pain subsided. In a couple of days, I was feeling much better and was able to walk without any discomfort. Dr. King instructed me to see a neurologist.

"Sure, sure," I said knowing full well I would procrastinate as long as possible. I didn't have time to see another doctor. I had too much work to do.

I felt very good and did not experience any more back pain. A couple months later, when the practice had a few slow days, Ellie persuaded me to make an appointment to see a neurologist at the Monroe Clinic in Monroe, Wisconsin, a nearby facility, which was staffed by doctors from the University of Wisconsin.

The neurological exam showed that there was a vast difference between the strength of one leg compared to the other. Since the problem didn't affect my daily routine, I was unaware of it.

An x-ray, called a mylogram, was needed to assist in a diagnosis. A contrast dye was injected into my spinal cord to see if any spinal discs were bulging and putting pressure on the nerves in my spinal cord.

The mylogram showed two huge lumps protruding into my spine from discs that were ruptured. I had to have back surgery. It was the only option for full recovery. Without the surgery, I could permanently damage the spinal cord and become paralyzed. Without procrastination, I made an appointment for the surgery as soon as possible.

After surgery, I woke up from the anesthetic with excruciating pain causing me to drift in and out of consciousness. My mother, who had not left my side, was able to get me to relax, and the pain subsided. After a while, Ellie went home to be with our kids, and my mother had left to get some rest.

Now alone, and fully awake, I began to wonder if the surgery had been successful. Since I have medical knowledge and am aware of anatomy, my mind conjured up all kinds of situations that could have gone wrong.

I needed to test my ability to move. I wiggled my toes - they worked. I moved my legs - they obeyed my instruction. I gently tried to move every joint in my body. By the time nurses came back to my room, I had gotten out of bed, walked to the bathroom and was shaving off the stubble that had grown on my face since the previous day.

The nurses were not outwardly pleased. With no one to support me, they were concerned that I could have fallen and injured myself. I was just happy I could walk.

The best way to regain strength was to exercise. I walked through pain and discomfort until I was told 'enough already'. You are going to collapse again. I think I shortened my hospital stay by pushing myself to exercise to the limit. In a week, I was ready to go back to work.

Tony Aurit, a high school senior, who was planning to go to college and study for a career in some type of medicine, had made calls with me before my surgery. We always had a good time together. I asked him to drive my truck when I started making calls again.

He tried to make the ride as smooth as possible, but every bump in the road would jar my recuperative back. When we arrived at a farm, Tony would carry the equipment into the barn. All I had to do was walk. I did not need physical strength to diagnosis problems.

Since I forced myself to keep moving, I healed rapidly. In a few months, I was able to work a full day.

27

The rainy spring made grass grow wildly, allowing grazers and other cattlemen to turn to their pastures for feed. We need rainy springs in southern Wisconsin to prepare for a good growing season.

There is a danger associated with fast growth spurts in our pastures, and unless we know the risks and prepare our animals, the consequences can be deadly.

Jason Rice had just started the evening milking and noticed 11 of his cows had not come into the barn from the pasture. He sent his teenage son to find them. The boy found the cows in the pasture, but they could not get up.

In a panic, Jason phoned our veterinary service for help. Adda alerted us to the emergency using the two-way radio system. Of the three veterinarians, I was the closest to Jason's farm. I was returning to town from another call and driving through a severe rainstorm, but since Jason's farm is located on a major highway, I told Adda I would be there in about 10 minutes.

Meanwhile, Jason called the office again. Adda was assuring him I was on the way when I pulled into his driveway.

"I can't afford to lose these cows." were Jason's first panicked words to me.

"Where are they?" I asked.

"Out in the pasture," Jason blurted.

"Take me to them," I said. I wanted to drive my four-wheel-drive truck, but the heavy rain had turned the lane into a quagmire of mud. I knew that if I tried to drive in that mud, I would get stuck.

"I guess we walk," I said dismally. The rain had not let up. We were going to get drenched. I gathered instruments and supplies that I would need from my truck. It was a lot of equipment, so Jason helped me carry it to the cows in the pasture.

We made our way down the lane. My boots were getting stuck in the mud. At one time, I almost walked right out of them. Both Jason and I stumbled and nearly fell before reaching solid ground.

One we reached the end of the lane, we looked into the pasture. We could see all 11 cows. They were laying in short grass and had good footing. All seemed to have gone down without struggling. They looked clean, and there was not any hoof marks in the grass surrounding the cows. Some looked depressed, and others looked anxious. Some cows were bobbing their heads as if too weak to lift them.

"What's wrong?" Jason pleaded.

My first concern was a diagnosis. I needed as much information as possible. I started examining the cows that were closest to me. I checked for fever and found they had a below normal temperature. I was able to get some urine, and it was normal. Respiration rates were above normal ranges. Those that were almost comatose had slow heartbeats, and those that appeared anxious were rapid, nothing unusual about that. There were very few clues for an accurate diagnosis. I decided to pursue a hunch.

"Jason, when did you turn these cows out to this pasture?" I asked.

"Two days ago," he replied.

"I think they have grass tetany," I replied.

"What's that?" asked Jason, bewildered.

I explained that fast growing grass could be deficient in magnesium. Magnesium is needed for nerve and muscle function. If absorbable magnesium is deficient, then the result mimics eclampsia or milkfever. Jason had no clue to understanding my scientific description about the condition of his cows. He did know that 11 of his cows were in danger of dying, and something needed to be done soon.

The rain was ending although the sky remained leaden. We had to slosh through the mud in the lane to get back to my truck. I needed to find all the magnesium products I had on board. I knew that my calcium products used for milkfever contained magnesium in sufficient amounts to help these cows. I could administer them intravenously, which would alleviate the symptoms quickly. Antacid boluses, another source of magnesium oxide, could also be used, but the reaction time would be slower.

Since I was working on a hunch, I began to doubt myself. What if my diagnosis was wrong? What had I missed? Could these cows be poisoned? Jason's worried attitude was becoming contagious.

Seeing all the drugs I wanted to transport to his cows, Jason suggested taking his tractor back down the lane to the pasture. He was sure it could make it down the lane, but probably not back up to the truck.

We loaded the tractor with the supplies, and off we went. I was trying to keep a handhold to balance myself and hold on to the drugs. It must have been a comical sight. Jason started to laugh at me. It helped eased some of his built up tension.

I instructed Jason to drive to the cow I considered nearest to death. I took a bottle of the intravenous solution and prepared to administer it, hoping it would help.

The liquid slowly drained from the bottle, and the cow started shaking. Usually, this phenomenon occurs just before death, but this cow was becoming more alert.

"Come on, baby," I whispered to her under my breath. Now definite signs of improvement were visible.

"I think we will be able to save your cows," I told Jason. I finished my treatment of the first cow and had started working on the second one. She, too, responded with signs of improvement. Fortunately, I had restocked my supply of the calcium and magnesium combination so that I had enough with me to treat all the cows. I even had enough magnesium boluses for all the down cows.

We were treating the last cow when the first one made an effort to get up. She stood after two tries. Jason started to smile, and clapped me on my back. The relief I felt, and Jason's smile made me realize how close a call this was. I was flying by the seat of my pants without any laboratory confirmation. Sometimes we have to trust our instincts. Usually the response to grass tetany is slower than for milkfever, but I wasn't complaining.

I told Jason to purchase grass tetany salt and to supplement the ration with magnesium. I returned later that day to check on the cows. All of them were in the barn, eating as though nothing had happened to them. The supplements prevented new cases from occurring. Grass tetany will no longer affect Jason's herd.

28

I felt confident I could handle almost any obstetrical problem with a cow, if I devoted time and energy to it. However, occasionally, a case would present itself that would deflate my ego and challenge my knowledge.

I was standing in front of a very large cow that was in labor trying to have a calf, but not really straining very hard. "A big cow like this should have no problems delivering a calf," I thought. "There should be plenty of room."

I pulled on a long plastic glove/sleeve that covered my hand and entire arm. I needed this protection to perform a rectal examination on the cow. Feeling thru the cow's rectum, I determined the unborn calf was dead and deteriorating inside the uterus. A vaginal exam determined that the cervix was contracted down on the calf's legs. I had enough experience in obstetrics to realize that the cow's life was in danger.

I briefly thought about the options and related them to the owner. There were only two, -- perform a caesarian section or let the cow die.

For some dairymen, choosing between the two alternatives becomes an economic decision. They consider the cost of the surgery, add in the cost of the downtime when the cow isn't producing milk and factor in the chances of survival. Which option will help increase the bottom line of his business?

For other dairymen, it is not that black and white. For example, does the animal have potential valuable genetics that would make her worth keeping? Is she a pet with emotional value? Expense is not considered when a pet's life is at stake.

Diane Miller looked at me with trusting eyes, "What would you do it if the cow was yours?" she asked.

Being ready to face the challenge and estimating the cow had a 50% chance of survival, I said, "I'd operate and do a C-section, if she were my cow." I love cows, too. Diane said, "OK, let's do it."

We led the cow to another building and due to her weaken condition, I decided to try a midline approach, which requires a long incision between the udder and the belly button. The cow must be lying on her back, which will position the uterus close to the incision. I gave the cow general anesthesia.

We flipped her on her back, and I prepped the surgical site. I had made a rather long initial incision when a loud pop occurred. My face was sprayed with a foul smelling red fluid, and then the cow died. Diane looked at me and questioned, "What happened?"

"I don't know but I am going to find out," I said. I made the incision deeper and longer. I found the fluid had come from the uterus, which had ruptured. I also discovered two dead decomposing calves instead of one. The uterus had filled with fluid and gas before rupturing and flooding the abdominal area.

Had this been my first case, I would have been devastated that the cow died. Now I observed her with wonderment. "It was amazing that she lived as long as she did under these circumstances," I said.

I washed myself, using generous amounts of soap and water, but I knew the odor would persist. My ego and self-esteem were bruised, but I would get over it. Diane seemed unfazed. I had tried to save her cow and that had satisfied her.

29

Al decided to end our six year partnership in Shullsburg Veterinary Service. He wanted to pursue other opportunities. I bought his half of the practice, and started looking for another veterinarian to work with me.

Dr. Charles Spurgeon was on a sight seeing trip through our area and stopped at the office to visit. Charley was a recent graduate of the University of Illinois School of Veterinary Medicine. After we talked for a while, he told me he was working in Iowa and was not completely satisfied with his job. I asked him if he wanted to work for me. He called a week later accepting my offer.

Charley was a tall, thin, lanky man never seen without his 10-gallon cowboy hat. The hat hid a head of blonde hair. He had a big mustache making him appear older than he was. In traditional cowboy style, Charlie owned and, occasionally wore a pair of six shooters in holsters on his belt.

On a personal side, Charlie was very friendly. He was socially friendly with many of our clients. However, he had a temper that made some clients uncomfortable. He was very knowledgeable in veterinary medicine, but he worked quickly, often not explaining what he was doing.

After a few years in Shullsburg, Charlie became restless and wanted to move out west. He bought a practice in the mountains of Utah.

Knowing that our practice in Shullsburg was more

than one man could handle, he started looking for his replacement. One of his classmates was working in a practice in Galena Illinois, which is not far from Shullsburg.

Charley introduced me to Dr. Ken Curtis. Charley speculated that Ken and I would work well together in veterinary practice. His prediction was quite accurate.

Ken came to interview me; I wasn't interviewing him. I think my philosophy, my goals, and my attitude about practice sold him on the idea that we could work well together. I admired Ken's frankness, his honesty, and knowledge. Ken is quiet, but when he speaks it's important to listen.

Ken is short and muscular, and I am tall and carry a few extra pounds. Ken has a beard, and I was clean-shaven. Ken likes to stay home, and I enjoy traveling. Ken is a hard worker trying to please clients, and I am a hard worker trying to please clients. Finally, I found a similarity. I was able to convince him to move to Shullsburg and work with me.

Ken and I have always discussed problems as they occurred. The bond that was established that first day remained throughout our partnership.

Our practice flourished and grew. Adda, Ken and I worked well together. Ken put down roots when he bought a farm. I made him a permanent partner. Communication, work ethic, and mutual respect remained the cornerstone of our practice.

Sadly, Charley Spurgeon developed terminal cancer a few years after he left Shullsburg. Before he died, he came to Shullsburg to visit Ken and I for the last time. I have fond memories of Dr. Spurgeon. Rest in peace, Charlie.

30

Cows do not have predictable appetites. Some research has indicated that the bovine would eat what its body required to remain healthy. If calcium was lacking in the diet, the cow would know to choose calcium from the buffet of feeds and supplements offered to her.

I don't think cows are that smart. I have a fondness for chocolate covered peanuts, and I eat many more than my body requires because they taste so good. If we assume that cows also eat what they enjoy, then the theory of cows eating what they need cannot be proven.

Several companies have sold cafeteria minerals. A row of boxes containing the various ingredients necessary to balance rations was offered to the cows. They would choose what they would like to eat. This concept never caught on, probably due to the chocolate covered peanut syndrome.

The boxes with the most palatable minerals were emptied first. Other minerals that didn't taste particularly good but were necessary for good nutrition, were not eaten.

To convince the cows to make the correct choices, flavoring was added to the less palatable minerals. That destroyed the premise of cows knowing what they needed.

Like people, animals sometimes eat what they shouldn't. They acquire peculiar tastes called pica and will eat almost anything.

Ralph Black phoned with a unique problem. He was one of the first dairymen in our area to expand his herd. To accommodate the extra cows, he used old buildings on his farm. He kept about fifteen 400-pound heifers in an old house that had been lived in by a previous owner.

When I arrived, Ralph waved me to the old house. "Hey, Doc. What do you think of this weather?" Ralph asked.

"It's a nice fall," I responded. The trees had lost their leaves and covered anything that had been left lying on the ground during the summer. Most of the crops had been harvested, and the temperature was in the 70's.

"What's up?" I asked.

"Take a look at these heifers and tell me what you see," he said.

I climbed over the fence that surrounded the yard and stared at the heifers. "I don't see anything unusual," I thought to myself. "Something must be going on that I hadn't observed".

Then I saw it. A heifer was trying to pass feces and couldn't. As I watched, I saw more animals straining. Their bellies seemed larger than normal.

"Well, Doc, tell me what's going on," he said.

"Are they eating?" I asked.

"No" he replied. I was baffled.

"I don't know," I responded truthfully.

"What do you suggest we do?" he asked.

"We load up that one," I pointed to a heifer, "and take her to Madison to the Veterinary School," I said.

"OK, make the arrangements," Ralph said.

I left the farm and drove to my office and made the telephone calls. Ralph took the heifer to Madison the next morning.

I received the diagnosis that afternoon. Soon after the heifer arrived at the large animal clinic and blood samples were drawn immediately. Everything appeared to be normal. Then the clinic staff noticed the extended abdomen and decided to do exploratory surgery. The rumen was enlarged, so they decided to open this stomach. They found black plastic sheeting, which was wadded into balls, inside the rumen. The balls obstructed the openings into the other stomachs, and the opening into the intestines. The digestive track was shut down.

"Other animals are showing similar symptoms. What should I do about them?" I asked the surgeon assigned to the case.

"Give them mineral oil," he suggested.

I went back to the farm and pumped mineral oil into all the heifers. Ralph and I raked some of the leaves that covered the yard around the old house to find the source of the plastic.

We discovered it in an old neglected garden, in a corner of the lot. The plastic probably had been used to cover an area to protect it from freezing. It had teeth marks left by the heifers when they bit off pieces. Why these animals ate this plastic, I will never know.

Several days passed before the mineral oil had an effect. Almost all the animals passed plastic balls covered with oil. They all resumed eating including the heifer that had the surgery. No other problems were encountered.

Plastic sheeting is inert and does not get absorbed. However, there are some petroleum-based products that can be absorbed.

Gary Anderson called with a problem affecting his 400-pound heifers. "What's wrong?" I asked getting out of my truck.

"Some of my calves broke down the gate that kept them out of my machine shed," he said. "I think they drank some old oil that was drained from the engines. I had it stored in five gallon pails."

We walked to the shed. Inside, I saw three buckets of oil had been spilled on the cement floor. There were small hoof prints everywhere. "Why do you think the calves drank this stuff?" I asked.

"Because otherwise they wouldn't be sick," he said, as if I had asked a stupid question.

We made our way to where the calves were housed. They appeared gaunt, their hair was raised, and they were uncomfortable. Some even demonstrated pain by kicking at their bellies. A closer exam revealed a black tarry material coming from the anus. This was not a diagnostic problem, but a treatment question.

Motor oil is toxic, destroying liver and kidney tissue. I was sure that the calves were jaundice. Jaundice describes a brownish color to mucous membranes such as tissue found around the eye and in the mouth. It is a sign of destroyed red blood cells that the liver is supposed to clear. It also occurs when there is so much red cell destruction that it overwhelms the normal liver function. In this case, I assumed liver destruction was from the used oil.

I pumped magnesium oxide into the calves to stop further absorption. I gave them all injections of B-vitamin complex to help the liver. I gave some of the severely effected electrolytes to treat dehydration from kidney damage. "Gary," I said. "I don't know if I helped or not."

"Well at least you tried," he said and clapped me on my back.

Several victims of the motor oil toxicity died. Others were sold because they had so much organ damage. The rest of the calves recovered completely and did not experience any detrimental effects. I think that the outcome was determined by the amount of oil consumed.

31

Ellie had attended a program called College Week for Women at the University of Wisconsin in Madison. When we were attending the University of Illinois, she hadn't found a course of study that was exciting and challenging. After attending this program in Madison, she discovered she loved working with computers and wanted to resume her education as soon as Judy started kindergarten.

I had a great many concerns. Who would take care of the kids if school was cancelled or if they became ill? Who would cook meals? Why should she have the freedom to pursue a personal goal, when I had to shoulder the entire responsibility of supporting the family? I hadn't considered the potential future benefits. I was thinking only of me.

The University of Wisconsin, Platteville is 22 miles from Shullsburg, and Ellie enrolled as a part time student. She declared a major in accounting and a minor in computer science. Ellie arranged her schedule to be home when the kids were out of school. The rest of the time, they were my responsibility.

I soon learned that having Ellie attend college was the best thing that could have happened to the Landau family. It gave me more responsibility with the children, and to my amazement, and I think theirs, we all became a closer family. Ellie and I were parenting as equals, and that was when I learned that our children were a real joy.

Since Ellie was doing something she really wanted, I decided to buy a motorcycle, something I had always wanted. It gave me an opportunity to cruise around the countryside in fresh air and solitude. I bought a 350 Honda, which turned out to be a little small for me, but perfect for Ellie. On nice days, she would take it to Platteville to attend her classes. She became known as 'MOTORCYCLE MAMA'. I kept telling her the bike was my toy.

Ellie's mother became ill with terminal brain cancer. One day, Ellie decided to take the motorcycle and visit her mom in the hospital in Rockford, Illinois, about 75 miles away. The weather was perfect, not a cloud in the sky. The temperature was a mild 60 degrees, wonderful for December. Ellie donned a snowmobile suit, heavy gloves, and a warm hat under her helmet. The miles zipped by. The open air made for an enjoyable ride and helped ease the sadness of the visit.

Ellie's dad came to the hospital for one of his two daily visits. Not wanting to worry him, she didn't tell him she rode the motorcycle from Shullsburg. About an hour later, Ellie glanced out of the hospital window and noticed storm clouds rolling in towards Rockford. She confessed to her dad that her mode of transportation was the bike, and she better leave immediately and head for home.

It started to drizzle. As she continued west, it began raining harder, and the temperature dropped. When she was 20 miles from home, the inside of her gloves became laden with water, and the rain was penetrating the snowmobile suit. She continued forging ahead slowly, extremely uncomfortable and scared.

She made it home safely, soaked to the skin and freezing cold. Ellie never rode that cycle again.

I, too, deemed it to be dangerous. I had a close call when my windshield and helmet visor fogged instantaneously, when I was returning from a quick trip to Dubuque. I nearly drove over an embankment. I was able to sell the cycle for what I had paid for it. I felt happy to see it go.

32

Spring breezes accompanied by a bright sun cause balmy and lazy days in Southern Wisconsin. It feels like the weight of winter has been lifted. The earth seems to awaken. I like to take things slow and easy on this kind of day, but Leo didn't let me.

Leo Porter was the envy of most of his neighbors. If he decided to put an addition onto his barn, expansion in the area was sure to follow. Leo made money when others were falling behind. He had the best cows in the county and kept utilizing good management techniques to continue to improve the herd. Cows did not stay on his farm unless they were heavy producers or genetically superior. Leo was also a very friendly person.

His call about a sick cow was not disturbing since this would provide me with an opportunity to discuss cows and be outside in the sun at the same time. I envisioned diagnosing and treating for 15 minutes and talking for 30 minutes.

I was greeted with the normal friendly 'hello' and led into the spotless milk-house. From there, we walked into the bright, freshly bedded barn.

Leo said, "Lilly is sick, and I have already sold her unborn calf."

"When is she due?" I questioned.

"In about 6 weeks," he said. "I have an offer of $40,000 for her."

He said it calmly, but I had a feeling of apprehension. "Why would a cow 6 weeks before calving get sick? Stress factors were at a minimum then," I thought.

Lilly wasn't too hard to pick out. She was getting up and down, kicking at her side, trying to ease the pain that seemed to consume her. My examination was made more difficult by the constant moving and kicking. This kind of pain can be attributed to a kidney stone making its way through a ureter or some twist of the gut. A kidney stone can pass, but the gut twist can be fatal to mom and baby. I thought the calf was too premature to do a C-section.

I heard it first through my stethoscope, the pinging of a displaced stomach. Between pain spasms, I heard it again. This time I was sure. We needed to determine our options. Leaving Lilly untreated was not one of them. She was suffering from a fatal right abomasal twist. The abomasum or fourth stomach of ruminants is similar to the stomach of animals with one stomach. The first three stomachs prepare food to be digested in the abomasum, making ruminants vegetarians and wonderful sources of animal proteins.

The abomasum is attached to the liver by a lacey thin membrane on one side called the lesser omentum. The other side has a loose, lacey, thin membrane that joins with the one wrapping the intestine and called the greater omentum. It is anchored near the spinal cord. This arrangement allows a lot of movement of the fourth stomach. If it turns on its long axis, a twist results near the duodenum, or opening into the small intestine. On the other side, a similar twist can be found at the opening of the omasum that leads into the abomasum. These twists can cut off the blood supply killing the cells of the abomasum. Gas is trapped, and more is formed, bloating the poor animal on the right side. The twists and the trapped gas causes the animal a great amount of pain. I explained the situations to Leo.

"Well, what do we do?" he asked.

"We operate and hope for the best," I said.

"What are her chances?" he asked morosely.

"Zip, if we do nothing, and slim, if we operate," I said.

I prepped Lilly and gave her enough anesthesia to stop her constant moving. I made my incision long enough to accommodate my hand and arm. I reached inside Lilly and confirmed my diagnosis.

I untwisted the abomasum and returned it into its proper position. Next, I took a handful of omentum, the lacey stuff near the pylorus, the valve that controls the opening of the stomach into the small intestine, and attached this to the outer wall near my incision.

I sutured the incision and hoped Lilly would survive. Surgery on a pregnant cow in her last trimester is not advised. High steroid levels in response to the stress of surgery can cause abortion of the calf. Intense pain can also lead to high steroid levels. I informed Leo of the poor survival rate of the mother and calf.

Lilly was fine the next day. She started eating and acting normal. She carried her calf to term and delivered a healthy bull that Leo had contracted. I felt like a hero. I saved the calf and the patient.

Two weeks after calving, Lilly was sick again. She was in severe pain, and I heard the pinging of a displaced stomach.

I operated again. The attachment to the wall to the abdominal cavity was still there, but the lacy thin membrane had thickened and felt like a two-inch rope. It had stretched from ¾ of an inch long to 2 feet long. The abomasum was twisted around it.

Lilly recovered the following day. "Looking good," I thought. I was wrong.

Lilly began to eat less and less yet she was getting bigger and bigger. She wasn't filling up with gas but something made her get bigger. It was water mixed with the little amount of food she had eaten. Her stomachs were not contracting, and food was not passed along. It remained trapped in her stomachs making her appear larger. She had vagal indigestion. The vagus nerve was stretched or injured due to the abomasal twists.

I referred Lilly to the University of Minnesota School of Veterinary Medicine where after a month of continual care, she was euthenized. They said my surgeries were OK, but the vagus nerve was destroyed. She had no chance. The vagus was injured due to stretching. A part of the nerve may have been involved in the twist.

The vagus can be injured from abscesses caused by hardware. Sharp objects may penetrate the reticulum or second stomach causing injury to the vagus. Injury can be caused from a butt or kick strategically placed. Even mounting, due to heat, may stretch this nerve.

Vagal indigestion can be easily overlooked when attempting to diagnose intestinal problems. It can be the cause of temporary indigestion or eating disorders that seem to be relieved by pills or other medication.

33

Ken and I soon needed help because we were overworked. We contacted Iowa State University for assistance in finding a recent veterinary graduate to fill our position. Tim Christopherson responded to our request. He was looking for a practice that did the majority of its work with dairy cattle. The location of our practice in southwestern Wisconsin was an added attraction for him. His parents lived in a town in eastern Iowa, and he would have a chance to visit with them on his days off.

We invited Tim to Shullsburg for an interview. He was tall, about six feet four inches and very slender. Curly black hair crowned his face. We enjoyed his great personality and realized during his first interview that he would be a great asset to our practice. We offered him the job before he left. After a short time, he called to tell us he would accept our position.

On the job training for new employees consists of riding with another veterinarian in order to become acquainted with the area, meet farmers and observe how we approached the different aspects of practice. Tim had been riding with Ken for a few weeks. Now he was with me in my truck.

The day was sunny and warm. We enjoyed working together. Tim was commenting on the surgery I had just performed. He had not seen the technique I had used. He was asking many questions.

We were concentrating on these new procedures when Tim happened to spot some people frantically waving. It appeared that they needed help. I turned the truck around and drove back to the commotion.

Two people were down in a septic tank and were in trouble. From above, looking down, it appeared that they were drowning. Emergency help was on the way. Tim couldn't wait. He found a ladder and was climbing down in the septic tank yelling at me to get a lariat for him to put around the victims.

By the time I ran to the truck and got back with the rope, the rescue squad had arrived. They immediately recognized the problem. The septic tank was full of methane gas. The two men cleaning the tank, and Tim, the good Samaritan coming to their rescue, had been overcome by the noxious fumes. All the rescue crew could do was pull out the three bodies from the tank. It all happened so fast.

Ken and I couldn't hire a new assistant for a number of years. We pushed ourselves and punished ourselves so the work would get done. All our energies went into our jobs. Somehow, this made it less painful. Punishing myself was wrong, but it was the only way I knew how to grieve for Tim.

It took a long time to recover from Tim's death. There never has been complete closure. He and his smile will live in my heart until it no longer beats. Until then, he is a remembered hero.

34

Formulating rations for our livestock is a cooperative venture. Appropriate supplements need to be added and rations balanced. Nutritionists create recipes that farmers need to follow. Dairymen put the ingredients together in a mixer. This process has potential for error.

Ingredients could be expensive, and the farmer may choose to ignore them. There often is an attitude that suggests 'this is the way I have always done it, and I haven't had problems'. That approach is dangerous.

Not only has the genetics of our herds changed, but so have the feeding requirements. We demand fast growth in our heifers and super performance in milk production. These goals do not allow dairymen to rely on luck. This case is one that proves the point.

My schedule on that rainy spring day included a visit to Irvin Hoskins's herd. Irvin was not a regular client. No one in the practice knew a lot about the herd. We didn't need to hurry, because the sick cow he wanted examined, hadn't eaten in two days. He had administered penicillin, and the cow hadn't improved.

I arrived at Irvin's farm about 2:00 p.m. that afternoon. He was busy cleaning calf pens when I found him. One pen he was planning to clean had quite a bit of manure and contained 16 Holstein heifers that weighted about 400 pounds. They were so crowded that there appeared to be no room for them to lie down.

"Take a look at these heifers," Irvin commented. "Aren't they nice?"

"Yes," I answered. "They are in good shape, but they need a lot more room."

Irvin was opening the gate of the pen as he told me about his sick cow. She was in his stanchion barn. My patient displayed a typical indigestion that would require a few rumen antacids tablets. I was thinking about the wasted antibiotics and the milk that had to be discarded, when I heard Irvin.

"Doc, Doc, come quick!" he yelled. I hurried to the pens where I had last talked to Irvin. The calves were out of their pens, and some were running around with abandon. They ran from one end of the barn to the other and then screeched to a halt. Some hit the wall, misjudging the distance needed to stop. It didn't seem to bother them. Others had serious problems. Three were dead. Several were lame and stiff. Two or three were down and couldn't get up.

"What's happening?" Irvin pleaded.

I didn't need or have time for lab confirmation. "Your calves are suffering from White Muscle Disease." I said.

"What are you talking about?" Irvin questioned.

"It's a vitamin E and selenium deficiency. Symptoms usually aren't this rapid, but the problem started much earlier," I explained.

Although some vitamin E is found in most feeds, our area is deficient in selenium. To insure proper levels, we need to supplement.

"Why did it happen now when the calves got out?" asked Irvin.

Muscle fibers that are deficient in vitamin E and selenium tend to turn white because calcium deposits in the tissue. These deposits interfere with muscle contraction. The large leg muscles often are involved causing lameness, stiffness, and the inability to get up.

Heart muscle is usually affected, causing damaged hearts. The hearts couldn't keep up with the demand the exercise created. A severe oxygen debt resulted, and the calves died.

The problem is much easier to prevent than treat. It takes a long time to mobilize the calcium deposits and remove the buildup. Some fibers die causing permanent damage to the muscles.

Recommended treatment is alpha tocopheral and selenium injections. Such preparations are available in concentrations for calves and older cattle. These products can be administered in dosage for treatment [therapeutic] or prevention [prophylactic]. Dosage schedules are listed on the bottle.

Selenium can be toxic. Too much can result in poisoning. It is usually advised that repeat treatment be done in monthly intervals. Since Irvin's calves needed immediate help, I administered the drug intravenously. I am not sure it made any difference. I also gave them cortisone to try to reduce inflammation caused by muscle damage.

Irvin thought he had caused the problem when he turned them out of the pen. They seemed normal. All of a sudden they were sick and dying. What a shock. The calves had not been off-feed or appeared sick.

I learned the calves were fed hay, ground corn and salt. The mineral mix contained only calcium and phosphorus. Added to the extreme overcrowding, the outbreak was a disaster waiting to happen.

Irvin would have realized that something was wrong if the calves had not been so crowded. He would have noticed a lame or stiff calf. He would have seen how slowly and painfully the calves got up.

No more had died when I visited the farm on the following day, but those affected hadn't improved. It took three weeks for the downed calves to get up. Some had a curved spine for the rest of their lives.

Irvin built bigger pens and supplemented the feed. He made sure that this problem would not be repeated.

But too much of a good thing can be toxic. Government regulations put a limit of how much selenium can be supplemented. The soil in our area is deficient in selenium, but certain areas of our country contain toxic levels.

35

Urine samples are part of examining a sick cow. A strip of treated plastic allowed to contact urine can identify a lot of problems. These strips have small areas coated with chemicals that can test the urine for pH, protein, glucose, ketones, and hidden blood. Other procedures can test for white blood cells, sediment and specific gravity.

The strip can detect high glucose. High glucose in a cow's urine suggests renal or kidney failure. Glucose is escaping and not filtered by the kidneys. It may mean that blood contains too much glucose, and the kidneys cannot absorb it all. This condition is called diabetes.

Cows that have high glucose are very sick. Insulin therapy has helped some of these animals. Once glucose levels go down, further treatment may not be needed. If the glucose does not go down, the cow usually dies.

The strip can detect high ketone levels. High ketone levels are common in sick cows. Any cow that doesn't metabolize glucose properly may develop ketosis. Glucose turns into carbon dioxide, water and energy after being metabolized. In ketosis, when not enough glucose is available, the breakdown is not complete and ketones are produced.

Ketones are toxic and may cause a cow to go 'off feed'. If a cow refuses feed because she doesn't feel like eating, more ketones are made and a vicious cycle is created. By not eating, cows cannot absorb the glucose.

In high producing dairy cows, where feed intake may not meet the high energy requirements of milk production, a shortage may develop, and ketosis is the result.

High ketone levels may impair brain function resulting in a nervous condition known as 'nervous ketosis'. Many of these cows act strange, pushing against their stalls, constantly licking foreign objects, and even acting blind. Some cows cannot get up and appear to have the symptoms of milkfever. Ketosis differs from milkfever, because it occurs much later after calving. Ketosis usually responds to intravenous glucose and steroids. Steroids mobilize glucose in the body and make it available for metabolism.

Occult blood is the last test on the strip. Blood may be obvious if it turns urine red. Occult means hidden and if blood exists, this test should find it.

Hidden blood usually indicates a urinary infection, which can be cured with antibiotics. Occult blood can be caused by kidney damage or bladder infection. A rectal exam can help to determine if the kidneys are damaged.

Retrieving a urine sample from a cow can be challenging. Usually the other cows are urinating but the sick cow is 'holding it'. Rubbing the area below the vulva and top of the udder, called the escutcheon, may stimulate urination. The cow usually humps up and goes. Others like the feeling of being rubbed there and move back and forth against the hand.

"What are you doing to my cow?" Linda wanted to know as she walked into the barn. I was trying to get a urine sample using the rubbing technique. Just then the cow humped and delivered a nice stream into my sample bottle.

"Oh", she said with a grin.

I had been called to Linda and Brad McArthur's farm to treat a sick cow. Ellie and I had seen Linda and Brad at a wedding a few months earlier. At the wedding reception, Linda had walked up to us and greeted me by saying, "Hi Doc. You know, this is the first time I've seen you with your clothes on."

Ellie laughed knowing what Linda had meant to say, but Brad couldn't believe his ears. "You really didn't say that, did you?" Quite embarrassed, Linda's face turned as red as her flaming red hair.

Quickly changing the subject before she made any more embarrassing comments, Linda asked about the cow. The strip indicated the cow had ketosis. After further examination, I found the cow also had a twisted stomach.

"When do you want to do surgery?" she asked. "I can help you now."

"OK," I said and headed toward the truck to get a surgery kit. Surgery took about an hour, and after we were done, Linda said, "I really didn't believe that the cow had a twisted stomach. I smelled her breath, and it smelled sweet and pungent. I have had other cows whose breath smelled sweet and pungent, and they only had ketosis not a twisted stomach."

"One test can often be misleading," I said. "Sometimes additional tests are necessary to establish a diagnosis." In this case, a urine sample was helpful, but was not diagnostic.

Another client, Ted Thomas called to tell me he was sure his cow, Georgia, had a twisted stomach. If I had the time, he wanted to do surgery that afternoon.

Ted kept sick cows in a pen. The cow he had confined was acting very strangely. She stood intently licking at the drinking fountain and was oblivious to anything else.

I walked up to her, and she didn't move. Getting a urine sample was easy because she was dribbling urine as she licked the fountain. The ketone strip changed immediately from pale yellow to a deep purple indicated a large amount of ketones spilling into her urine from her kidneys. I checked her for a twisted stomach.

"Can't hear a twisted stomach, Ted. Georgia appears to have nervous ketosis not a twist. We'll check her again in the morning," I said after the physical exam.

"That should save me some money," Ted said as we restrained the cow. I administered intravenous glucose. By the next morning, the cow had stopped licking, was eating and seemed normal. I listened again for a displaced abomasum and couldn't hear one. Georgia had a case of nervous ketosis due to limited glucose intake.

36

Rectal exams of cows may seem to be unappealing, but, to me, the procedure was necessary, productive and important. Cows don't mind the intrusion, and very little, if any, injury occurs during the process.

Rectal exam are great diagnostic tools. Pelvic and abdominal cavities can be examined thru the intestinal wall. Many of the internal organs can be felt. The left kidney, the rumen, the reproductive tract, some blood vessels, intestines, and bladder can be palpated during the exam.

"My prize cow, Sara, hasn't been herself for about a week," Reggie Post said as I picked up the office phone.

I remembered Sara. She produced a lot of milk, but that was her only good quality. I was feeling apprehensive about this call as I drove to the farm. Sara was one of those rare Holsteins who doesn't like humans. She was a skittish and nervous cow whose head would go up the moment I walked into the barn. I could not anticipate how she would react to my poking and prodding which was necessary for an examination. Cows normally protect themselves by kicking and head butting, but Sara was not normal. She would swing away with her hind feet when I just walked near her.

"Doc, my man," Reggie greeted me as he came around the corner of a building. "Sara is waiting for you," he said grinning and making me feel uncomfortable as we entered his barn.

Sara stood in her stall with head down seeming to pay no attention to me. Normally, she would hold her head high in the air, eyes wide, and blazing, snorting and pawing at the ground with her front feet.

Sara didn't even try to attack during the physical exam. However, after doing the routine examination, I didn't have a clue as to what ailed Sara.

"Got to do a rectal," I said to Reggie. I went to my truck for a lubricated glove that had a long sleeve that comes to my shoulder. I went back to Sara and gingerly introduced my protected hand and arm into her rectum. Uncharacteristically, Sara didn't move.

She groaned as I touched her left kidney. It was swollen, enlarged and very painful. "I know what's bothering her," I said.

Reggie looked at me and as if reading my mind said, "You don't like this cow much, but you have to fix her if you can."

"OK," I said, "she has kidney infection. The medical term for this problem is nephritis."

"So your telling me Sara has nephritis, but you haven't told me what to do about it," Reggie said. "Getting information from you about how to treat Sara is a hard job," he added.

"I'm sorry but I don't think dangerous cows are worth keeping, and Sara is dangerous," I said. "She might respond to antibiotics. For some cows with nephritis, antibiotics can be a temporary treatment, but it comes back. Each attack is worse. Sara needs antibiotic shots once a day for at least a week. The first one may make her feel better, and then she'll get mean again. How can you get all those injections into her without getting hurt or killed?"

Reggie seemed stunned at what I had just said.

"And another problem," I continued. "If you plan to sell her without treatment, she will be condemned at slaughter, and if she responds and relapses, she will be condemned for having antibiotics in her system."

"Wow, I didn't think of all that," Reggie replied and then added, "Here I thought you weren't giving me all the information because you don't like Sara."

I didn't respond to that comment.

I still wasn't sure if Sara's condition was acute or chronic. If it was acute or had suddenly occurred, Sara would survive this attack, but be more vulnerable to new ones. If the condition was chronic, or had been going on for sometime, Sara would just continue to decline and die. Due to her aggressiveness, it was hard to determine when or if she had been ill prior to this visit.

"Here is what happens with nephritis. The kidneys act as filters. Blood enters them at high pressure, and the tubes of the kidneys remove waste and toxic materials absorbed from the intestine. Chronic nephritis can be caused from high blood pressure, damage from absorbed toxins, or damage of renal tissue. Infections can create both acute and chronic disease. Kidney infection can be caused from bacterium traveling from the bladder and into the kidneys or bacterium from blood."

"More information than I want to know or can understand," Reggie said. "Just tell me what I should do?"

"Give her penicillin and see what happens," I answered.

"Sounds like a plan," Reggie said.

Sara responded to the first injection, and Reggie injected her again the second day. By that time, Sara had physically improved. Making her feel better was a double-edged sword. Sara had regained the fire in her eyes, and her mean spirit was back. She wouldn't let anyone near her including Reggie. She could not be milked.

Before the 30 -day antibiotic withdrawal period had passed, Sara got sick again. Reggie gave her more antibiotics, but the response was shorter and less dramatic. Sara died about two months later.

"I'm selling Sara's off-spring," Reggie said to me after Sara had died. "I don't want to deal with 'crazy' cows again," he added.

"YES!" I cheered silently as I walked out of the barn.

37

All warm-blooded animals are susceptible to clostridium infections. Clostridium organisms are found in soils and on objects that can penetrate skin. Although a number of names apply to the diseases that they cause, the bacteria are related. These cousins have a lot in common. As long as they are actively growing, they are not destructive. Upon death of the germ, lethal toxins are released. Diseases these organisms cause include blackleg, tetanus, malignant edema, botulism, gangrene, enterotoxemia and other infections that lead to sudden death. Most deaths occur in younger animals due to inadequate immune response.

This family of organisms is usually anaerobic meaning they can only grow in an environment devoid of oxygen. The toxins they produce cause tissue death, by interfering with blood supply. Some are gas producers, forming pockets of gas that have very distinct odors. Carcasses often appear bloated due to the gases released. Sometimes only one animal has symptoms. Other times many animals in a herd are sick. It depends on the source of infection and the resistance of the animals.

When I worked in the equine practice in Barrington, I saw a lot of tetanus in horses. Any wound that penetrates a horse's skin can be a source of tetanus organisms. Clostridium Tetani resides in the gut of horses as part of the normal flora. Horses need to be protected with vaccination or given tetanus antitoxin after a wound.

Clostridium Chauvei causes blackleg in cattle. The bacteria produce toxins in large muscle groups. Symptoms may start as lameness followed by sudden death. Cattlemen usually find dead animals with gas bubbles under their skin. Young animals need to be vaccinated.

My first encounter with blackleg was in a valuable black Angus bull. He was found dead in a pasture. The owner had observed the bull the night before, grazing with no apparent problems. The next day, he was dead. The tissue under the skin was swollen with gas bubbles.

I cut a small hole through the skin that allowed a small amount of gas to escape. It smelled like rancid butter. The symptoms pointed to a textbook case of blackleg. I instructed the farmer to vaccinate all his cattle that were under two years old. For an additional safeguard, I told him to move them to a different pasture.

The farmer followed my advice, and no more deaths occurred. The problem seemed solved.

My second encounter with blackleg made me question my knowledge. John Grimes phoned our office with a puzzling problem. He had just come from his heifer pasture and had found 8 yearlings dead. They were put in the pasture the week before with no apparent problems. He checked them regularly, every other day, and had not seen any potential problems. This morning he had found the results of an invisible killer.

I left the office immediately and drove to John's farm. He was waiting at the pasture gate. He looked worried; wondering how many more heifers would die. The dead heifers were scattered around his 60-acre pasture. A large creek flowed through the center of the field, and the dead animals were lying on both sides of the stream. A torrent of rain had caused the water of the creek to flood and spill over its banks during the previous week. After the storm, the water had receded. The water level was normal, now, but traces of disturbed grass and weeds remained on the banks of the stream.

I drove to the closest dead heifer. She was bloated with legs and feet in the air. I drove around the pasture looking at the other dead animals. They all were bloated with legs and feet in the air.

It seemed unlikely that so many had been exposed to and died from a Clostridium disease. Yet, all the classic physical evidence was there

There were 15 heifers that were still alive and seemed normal. I told John to move them to a different pasture and inject them with penicillin and Clostridium vaccine. If any of the normal appearing animals were harboring the bacteria, penicillin would kill the organism. The vaccine would trigger the animals to produce their own immunity.

We loaded two of the dead carcasses in a pickup truck. I wanted to post one and send the other one to the state lab in Madison to confirm my diagnosis. When performing the autopsy, I was careful not to contaminate the ground or the truck. I made a small hole in the carcasses. There was a release of gas with the odor as rancid butter. I was sure the heifers had died of Clostridium Chauvoei.

Lab results confirmed Clostridium Chauvoei. Since none of John's remaining heifers became sick, I thought I had the perfect solution to blackleg.

John came to the office two weeks later questioning me about moving the heifers back to the other pasture?

"Well, they were vaccinated and should have some resistance," I commented.

"That's good enough for me," John replied.

"I am not sure the vaccine has given them total immunity to blackleg," I said hesitantly. "Can't you put them somewhere else?"

"I need the room," John said as he walked out of the door.

Two more heifers died after they were put back in the contaminated pasture. The flood probably swept the organisms into the pasture and caused a high enough concentration to make the area around the creek lethal. John moved the healthy calves to a different area permanently and converted the pasture into a cornfield.

Manufacturers of modern killed vaccines suggest two doses two weeks apart. This procedure helps to bolster the immune response. However, if the dose of toxin exceeds the protection provided by the vaccine, the animal will die. We routinely vaccinate for blackleg even if the disease has not been diagnosed on the farm.

38

Most dairy cattle caretakers are familiar with downer cows. They are the frustrating ones who are unable to get up or walk. Downer cows are often misunderstood. They are thought to be stubborn and just don't want to get up. The afflicted cow requires a great deal of the dairyman's time, and the prognosis is dubious. A satisfactory outcome is only achieved when the cow stands and walks to the bunk to eat.

Most studies show that the cause of downer cow syndrome is trauma. It can be attributed to numerous conditions. Cow comfort is important, because cows need to get up and down without restriction. Nutrition plays a key role by supplying energy and minerals for proper muscle control and bone structure. Bedding has to be considered so the cows are dry and can lie down without exposure or pressure on their legs and body.

Cows that are too fat or too thin are candidates for this syndrome. Separating dry cows from those that are lactating has made a huge difference in some herds.

Slippery footing can injure cows. Wet cement or ice can create a surface that leads to cows doing the splits, which can break the back leg at the thin part of the femur bone. Cows with these kinds of fractures lie on their briskets in great pain.

Obterator paralysis can cause downer cow syndrome. This condition is usually seen in first calf heifers after giving birth to large calves. The pressure the calf applies to the nerves in the pelvis, and the length of time that the pressure persists, determines the severity of the paralysis.

Research has proven that a bovine cannot lie in one position very long. Rolling such an animal from side to side can help lessen the paralysis.

I have treated a lot of animals for milkfever or eclampsia in my bovine practice. Some of these cases became downer cows. I often found milkfever cows in lateral recumbence, lying on their side, not moving. A couple bottles of calcium gluconate given very slowly, by intravenous injection would improve their condition dramatically. They would quickly shake off the stupor and usually be able to get up in a short time.

Problems with downer cows caused from milkfever usually start later in the day. Greg Halprin called with just such a senerio. I had treated the cow early in the morning, and she was still down in the late afternoon. Greg was a fine manager. He kept his barn clean, and his cows were well fed. His barn had two rows. One row was stanchions, and the other row had tie stalls. Each row held 30 high producing Holstein cows. Greg took well-deserved pride in his herd.

The cow I had treated in the morning had calved before her due date. Greg usually put cows that were about to give birth in a stall. The stall for this cow was ready. It had been washed, and new, deep bedding had been added for the impending arrival. Greg planned to follow all the procedures of good management. However, because she delivered early, the cow was still in her stanchion.

She had made no attempt to get up since the morning treatment. She hadn't moved at all. She did manage to roll and turn so now both hind legs were trapped in the gutter. They were wedged so tightly that we couldn't move them. Greg and I tried to roll the cow to free her legs, but she was too big. Since she appeared depressed, I decided that one more treatment for milk fever would make her more alert, and she could help us.

The calcium did have an effect. As we prodded her, and she attempted to get up, we heard a sickening 'POP' sound. Greg looked up and gave me a questioning glance.

My stomach churned, and I was swept with a wave of nausea. My face must have turned a ghostly white. "What's the matter with you, Doc?" Greg asked.

"The 'POP' sound was breaking bone. Her leg is fractured." I managed to stammer. "Let's move her out of the barn and make her as comfortable as possible." Somehow, it wasn't fair. We had worked so hard to help this cow get up without further complications.

Occasionally, I come in contact with struggling farmers. A few weeks later, a farmer called our office for the first time. All he said was that he had some cows down. The message was very vague, especially from a new client.

The farm was hidden from view by a large hill, and the lane going to it was a small drive, which could easily be missed from the main road. As I turned toward the farmstead, I saw an old ramshackle barn that needed paint and structural repair. The farmhouse was also deteriorated. I was concerned that people were actually living in that house.

The owners met me at the milk-house, apprehension on their faces. I followed the farmer into the barn and stared at some of the thinnest animals I had ever seen.

"What are you thinking, treating animals like this?" I questioned in a very harsh manner. The couple became distraught as I continued to ask more questions. I wanted to find out what happened before I called in the authorities.

Between sobs, they told me they didn't have any money to buy feed for the cows or food for themselves. Somehow, I needed to find feed for the animals fast. Half the cows didn't have enough energy to stand.

We located all the remaining edible feed stuffs available on the farm and fed it to the cows. I made some calls to clients who lived near by. They volunteered to deliver feed for the animals and bring some food for the people who were living on the farm.

I had the farmer call an auctioneer to get an appointment to have the cows sold as soon as possible. The feed from the neighboring farmers would be paid for by the proceeds of the sale.

The cows were sold at an auction, my volunteers got paid, and the people on the farm moved away.

It is a privilege to own and take care of animals, farm animals and pets alike. We need to make sure that our animals are loved, protected and fed. Every client I worked with understood this basic element of human caring

39

A Bar Mitzvah (masculine) or a Bat Mitzvah (feminine) is a life cycle event for 13-year-old Jewish children. The translation, "student of the commandments", identifies the person as an adult in the tenets of the Jewish religion. It requires dedication on the part of both the teacher and the student.

Ellie's dad, Sol Burstein, or Grandpa Sol, a pillar in the Jewish community of Rockford, Illinois, made a commitment to instruct each of our children in the cantillations of the Hebrew scripture. He coached and cajoled them to enunciate each Hebrew word and chant the 'parsha' fluently. He dedicated a great deal of time to prepare them for their solo presentation on the day of their Bar or Bat Mitzvah.

In order to teach the kids, Grandpa drove 75 miles to Shullsburg, two nights a week. Upon Grandpa's arrival, we had supper, and then the soon-to-be 13 year old child would have his or her lesson. When the lesson for the evening was over, there would be a few games of ping-pong. Grandpa was a very good ping-pong player and would not ease up to allow anyone to beat him. After the ping pong games, he would drive 75 miles back to Rockford so he could go to work the next day.

Grandpa Sol was about 5' 10", but he gave the impression of being much taller. He stood straight, shoulders back, and was in excellent physical shape. He exercised by walking very fast. His graying hair and dark brown eyes made him quite formidable. He could be very charming, but with me, he was stern and somewhat stiff. I suspect that he considered me unworthy of his beautiful and intelligent daughter.

As the oldest grandchild, Debbie was Grandpa's first Bat Mitzvah student. She studied hard to learn the material, and wanted to please her Grandfather with her progress. She seemed excited about seeing his car pull up to our house for her lesson. He must have been tired after a full day of work, but he never showed it. After dinner, Debbie and Grandpa would go into the living room by themselves for the study time. My daughter became quite knowledgeable and spiritual during this learning process.

Her Bat Mitzvah service was in May, shortly before her 13th birthday. Friends and relatives came from all over the country to help our family celebrate this happy occasion. Debbie did an excellent job with her Hebrew reading. Ellie and I were very proud of her.

Steve didn't have the same kind of dedication or motivation. He was not excited to see his Grandpa's car drive up to our house. After dinner, Steve would take tiny steps to get into the living room for his lesson. We dubbed his procrastination, "The Bar Mitzvah Shuffle". He definitely tried Grandpa's patience.

Grandpa had a plan that he hoped would motivate Steve. He wanted ME to learn to read and chant one of the seven Torah sections at Steve's Bar Mitzvah. "He's your son and you owe him this," Grandpa said. The plan seemed to work. Steve took more interest in his studies, since he knew I was being subjected to the same mental challenges.

Even though Steve was blasé during every lesson, he did want to do a good job to please his grandfather. While Grandpa was teaching him one Torah section twice a week, Steve was secretly learning a second Torah section from a tape which Ellie's brother, Mickey, had recorded. Ellie would help Steve with the Hebrew, and Mickey would do some coaching over the phone. Steve wanted to surprise and honor his grandfather by chanting an extra Torah portion.

Everyone gathered for the big event in the small Temple in Dubuque, Iowa. Family and friends came from many regions of the country. Steve and I chanted our planned parts flawlessly. Now, it was time for the part that Grandpa thought he was scheduled to do.

Just before Grandpa began the reading, Steve reached for the *'yad'* or pointer used in reading the Torah. Quietly Steve told Grandpa he was going to do this part in his honor. First amazement crossed Grandpa's face followed by tears of happiness as Steve started chanting the words. I never saw Grandpa so emotional. He could not believe his challenging student had mastered an additional part of the service just for him.

When it was David's turn to study for his Bar Mitzvah, he was familiar with the procedure. He was a fast learner and worked hard, but was the brunt of teasing from Steve, who was now 15 years old. His kid brother was now stuck with the twice weekly lessons. Grandpa saw thru the 'brotherly love' hazing and came up with a plan. Since there were seven parts of the Torah to be chanted, he decided Debbie, Steve, Ellie and I would also have parts in David's Bar Mitzvah reading. We all had study sessions with Grandpa. Everyone had parts to learn, so no one could tease or be teased.

David's 13th birthday on the Hebrew calendar fell during the 2nd week of January. Weather in Wisconsin in January is unpredictable, but Ellie wanted to have the Bar Mitzvah at that time rather than waiting until spring. The weather turned out to be beautiful, no clouds and a strong sun. It was an ideal day.

Family and guests stay at a Dubuque hotel for the weekend. Ellie, Steve and I had gone to the Temple for some last minute preparations. We hurried back to the hotel to dress for dinner and the evening service. We were meeting our guests in the hotel restaurant. I dropped Steve off at the lobby door with instructions to quickly get cleaned up and meet everyone else in the restaurant. Ellie remained with me when I parked the car.

We walked into the lobby and found the power had just gone out. Hotel maintenance was attempting to find the reason. We had to walk up the stairs to our room. This was a major inconvenience, since we were late and our guests would be waiting.

We quickly changed our clothes and walked down the stairs to the dining room. Everyone was *'kvetching'* about no electricity and having to walk down the stairs. I mentally did a head count and realized one person was missing. Steve wasn't there! He was staying in Grandpa's room, but Grandpa hadn't seen him all afternoon. That made sense, since he was with us until I dropped him off at the lobby door when I went to park the car.

We managed to regain some rational thinking. What could have happened to Steve from the time we left him off at the door of the hotel? Ellie and I were less than 5 minutes behind him walking into the hotel. He would have walked into the hotel and got in the elevator to go to his room. THE ELEVATOR -- NO ELECTICITY!

I ran to the door of the elevator shaft and yelled as loud as possible, "STEVE, are you in there?"

A muffled voice came back. "I'm stuck in here. The door is open a crack, but I can't get out."

I ran up six flights of stairs to where the elevator was stuck. Steve had remained calm, knowing he would be rescued. Hotel maintenance was able to get the door opened. It was the longest ten minutes of my life.

David's Bar Mitzvah was a huge success. The congregation enjoyed the participation of the entire family, and David chanted his part flawlessly

Judy loves performing, so her Bat Mitzvah was easy. Again, the entire family participated. Judy was thrilled to stand up in front of the congregation chanting her Torah portion and delivering her speech. Grandpa beamed as his last Landau pupil recited Torah. He had completed his self-made commitment to assist his grandchildren through one of the major Jewish life cycles events

40

Farmers and veterinarians often question the feasibility of vaccinations. Does it do any good? Is it cost effective? Are they worth the expense? Would another procedure make more money?

As the liquid containing the vaccine leaves the syringe, goes through the needle, and into some part of an animal, I question whether I have, in any way, helped in preventing disease. The animals receiving the vaccine must develop an immune response. Some animals cannot become immune. They do not have the capacity to recognize the antigens or foreign protein that are the components of vaccines.

Sam Jones, a new client, phoned our veterinary office to tell us he had a sick cow. He was not going to be at the farm, because he had errands to run, but he would identify her with an orange marker. Since I didn't know the owner, his presence seemed important to me. Leaving a note cannot convey what I want to express. Also, it is impossible to obtain a good history when the owner or someone else familiar with the herd is not there. However, I would check the condition of the cow on my own.

I included the visit on my list of calls and decided to make it in the late morning when I was in the neighborhood. The farm, nestled in a grove of trees, was at the end of a long lane. It was isolated and beautiful.

The old barn needed paint, but still seemed well maintained. I entered it through the milkhouse.

The cows were tied in old wooden stanchions. There were short rows of cows facing each other separated by the stanchions, the typical setup of barns dating back to the 1930's.

As my eyes adjusted to the darkness of the barn, I was struck with awe. The animals staring back at me were gorgeous. Each one displayed a perfect square udder and were in such good body condition, that it took my breath away. I wanted to meet Sam and congratulate him for a job well done.

I began my examination of the cow with the orange mark by taking her temperature. It was elevated, about 4°. She appeared to be drooling excessive saliva from her mouth and clear discharges were coming from her eyes.

Warning bells were going off in my mind. As if on cue, the cow turned her head to look at me, and in her eyes, I saw a desperation that still haunts me today. It was a cry for help! I needed to make a diagnosis. I had a suspicion, but I needed more evidence.

The cows next to the identified one were not normal either. They, too, were drooling and not eating all the feed that was in front of them. Their temperatures were elevated. The condition was not affecting just one cow. Other cows had the same symptoms. I had justification to be very concerned.

I needed to talk to someone who knew the cows and their history. I was aware of another Jones' farm in the area. I went there hoping the man was a relative.

The man was Sam's father. He told me Sam had just purchased the cows to start his own milking herd.

"Was this a completely closed herd?" I asked, trying to find out if these cows had been completely isolated from any other cows.

"Yes," he answered.

I told him I thought the herd had a viral infection called BVD or Infectious Bovine Diarrhea. If BVD was the problem, then the prognosis was not good. This herd had not been protected by vaccination.

It was important to know if any other cows had been brought in to add to the herd. I asked my previous question a different way. "Has Sam brought any new cows to the farm."

"No, not really, unless you want to count the two heifers he bought a couple weeks ago," he replied. "But, they were vaccinated."

I thanked him for the information. He had given me a big clue to the cause of the illness. I asked him to tell Sam that I would be back the following day to recheck the cows.

Vaccinated animals can still have a virus. They may become slightly ill, but not show distinguishing symptoms. They could be the source of infection and spread it to the unvaccinated animals. I went home to change clothes and disinfect everything I had used.

I was really hoping for improvement when I returned the next day, but what I found confirmed my diagnosis. The cow I had examined the day before still had the same fever despite antibiotics and several others were showing diarrhea. The two new heifers were standing in their stanchions chewing their cud without a concern in the world. A virus infection does not respond to antibiotic treatment, so, all I could do was support the sickest with fluids and aspirin, and wait the outcome of the disease. I took blood samples to substantiate my diagnosis, but I was convinced that we were dealing with BVD brought to the farm by those two heifers.

I returned everyday to try to help those in trouble. My first patient developed diarrhea, and I tried to assist her. Her temperature went down, and the diarrhea seemed to get better. She became interested in her feed. Unfortunately BVD is diphasic, meaning that the first viremia, or release of virus into the blood, had been overcome, but another batch was about to be released. Several days passed before she became sick again, and the poor cow that asked me for help with her big brown eyes, died.

This bunch of cows had impacted me emotionally. I had done the best I could, and it was not enough. I am writing this story with tears in my eyes because I still remember the exquisite looking herd of cows I saw on my first visit to the farm.

The virus had run its course after a few weeks. Sam had lost one-third of the herd. Most of the cows that were pregnant had aborted their calves. Sam had to sell the cows that had survived because the bank wouldn't extend his loan.

The two vaccinated heifers remained disease free. I have always wondered what would have happened if the herd had been vaccinated. Vaccinations help prevent outbreaks of disease.

41

Johne's is a major disease among bovines. The
organism responsible is related to tuberculosis.
Heinrich Albert Johne discovered Mycobacterium
paratuberculosis, the organism responsible for the
disease, in the late 1800's. It is a very resilient
bacterium almost impossible to treat. The organism
lives in a white blood cell that transports it to the target
organ, the large intestine. Once there, it damages
structures of the large intestine causing untreatable
diarrhea.

Chris Baldwin had a sanitation problem. His
milking parlor was always clean, but the free stalls,
where the cows were housed, were in terrible condition.
Ventilation was poor, water dripped from the ceiling
causing the cement floors to be slippery and wet.
Everything was always damp. In the winter, ice
covered the floor making it difficult to remove manure.
In addition to these problems, his manure holding
system, a large holding tank was not big enough, and it
overflowed. All these deficiencies caused a perfect
environment for Johne's disease.

Amazingly, Chris's herd remained healthy. Aside
from some traumas from slipping and some respiratory
infections, the herd managed to be profitable.

Chris was planning to replace all these structures
with a modern dairy. Plans had been drawn and
improvements were coming. He was going to include a
sick room with a head chute for me to treat any sick
animals. It would have a place for instruments that

would make surgery a delight. I would no longer need to climb over pails and bales of straw. I could hardly wait. So far, nothing had been started. Chris was waiting for loan approval.

I received a call from Chris stating he had a problem with a bull that he had purchased a couple years before. Chris wanted to use him to breed heifers in a pasture some distance from the farm.

I was puzzled. Treating a bull in a pasture is nearly impossible. Usually bulls are large, and this one was free to roam in the pasture. He definitely won't stand still for me to examine him. He might decide he doesn't like me and try to hurt me. I asked Chris, "How do we handle a bull in a pasture? I'm not much of a cowboy!"

"We can drive right up to him, and you can see him from your truck. You don't have to get out. Just look at him and give me an opinion," he replied testily.

I couldn't understand why Chris just wanted me to see a bull and not treat him. I decided to drop my opposition and do what I was asked. The pastures were dry, and the summer heat had turned mud to a hard dry surface that could easily support my truck.

Chris got in the truck, and I drove to the pasture. "What's going on with the bull?" I inquired since his request was very unusual, and I didn't know what to expect.

"See for yourself, and you tell me what you think." Chris said.

"Why was Chris being so evasive in answering my questions," I wondered. Everything appeared to be secretive.

The pasture contained a small creek, and standing on the bank was the bull. The poor creature was a skeleton covered with skin. Bones protruded everywhere. I was

surprised that he still had enough energy to stand.
"Why didn't you called earlier?" I asked.

"I thought he would improve." he replied.

"Improve from what?" I asked.

"The diarrhea," he answered.

I looked at the tail of the bull, which was smeared
with signs of severe diarrhea. It looked as if the bull
was passing brown water. He didn't have enough
energy to raise his tail.

"Have any heifers calved that were bred to this
bull?" I questioned.

"Yes. They are not doing well. Some of them have
continual diarrhea too. I had to sell some of the poor
producers," he said. "They fell apart after calving. I am
very disappointed with this bunch."

Chris wanted a cure. He didn't want to hear what
I was about to tell him, even though he knew what
these symptoms implied.

I needed fecal samples to substantiate my
diagnosis of Johne's. Manure was the only reliable
sample I could submit for confirming a Johne's
diagnosis. Blood tests had not been perfected when this
problem was occurring.

The turn around process for testing was six weeks
from the time the lab received the sample to the time
the results were known. It seems like an eternity.

Not only were more heifers getting diarrhea, but
now cows were showing symptoms as well. This was a
major problem without any positive solution. Finally,
the lab results came back confirming the herd was
infected with Johne's.

Chris was losing money. The bank would not
finance a herd infected with Johne's. Chris planned to
have a sale to recover some of his losses. If there were
to be an auction, the disease would spread. Thinking of

the consequences to other herds, I suggested sending them to be slaughtered, which only resulted in infuriating Chris. He was the person that would be suffering a financial crisis.

At the time, two neighboring states did not have any restrictions against the importation and sale of a known Johne's positive herd. The sale took place and was advertised as a known infected herd. The cows were sold for near slaughter prices. Many of them went to other farms and sale barns.

I look back on this experience as a no-win situation. I question if I could have done more. Chris still doesn't talk to me. He still thinks that I had turned against him.

Johne's is more prevalent now than at the time when Chris had his problems. Chris wasn't an isolated case. Other dairymen were forced to sell their animals, and the disease spread. Laws have been passed to prevent the sale of infected herds, but the disease has not been eradicated.

Good sanitation and ventilation keep symptoms to a minimum, but cows carry the germ. Blood tests, with two to three day turn-around, are now available and can determine if a cow is a carrier. Carriers can be eliminated, and herds can be certified free of Johne's. Replacement cows can be purchased from tested herds with the knowledge that chances of infection are greatly reduced.

42

Seven and a half years after announcing to me that she was going to go back to college, Ellie reached her goal and graduated with a degree in accounting and computer science. Our entire family attended her graduation ceremony. When her name was read to walk across the stage to accept her diploma, four enthusiastic voices yelled, "THAT'S OUR MOM!"

"What should I do now that I have my degree?" Ellie asked innocently.

I had anticipated this question, but I had to be diplomatic. Any answer on my part would be wrong, so I responded with a question. "What would you like to do?" I asked as if I didn't already know.

"Get a job," she answered, and with that we became a double income family. Ellie got a job with her first interview and went to work for a computer software company in Dubuque, Iowa. Subsequently, she had a position with a software company located in Chicago. She worked as a remote employee with her office in our home and traveled to client sites whenever necessary.

Her work enabled us to educate our four children. It has given us financial security. As I always tell her, "You were right, and I was wrong."

43

The storm was unexpected and severe. Lightening
filled the sky on this summer day, late in the afternoon.
It disappeared about as fast as it had approached
leaving a glistening landscape as the sun came out
ready to set and disappear giving way to night.

As usual, I was out making visits to sick cows
when my radio came to life with Adda's voice. Adda
had a message from Derrick Kutz, a client located close
to Shullsburg, who had found four dead heifers in a lot
across the road from his buildings. He wasn't surprised
because lightening had been flashing continuously in
the area, and the deaths were probably due to lightening
strike. A logical assumption, and since it was getting
dark, we postponed the visit until early the next morning.

On my way home for breakfast after an early
morning obstetrical case, I stopped at Derrick's.
Derrick was milking, and his wife, Monica, showed me
the dead heifers in a 10-acre pasture. Out of a group of
15 six-month-old animals, four had been killed. They
were scattered in different areas of the pasture.
Lightening usually kills animals that are clustered
together, because the electricity jumps from one to
another, thereby, electrocuting all of them. This scene
did not resemble a lightening strike.

I decided to perform an autopsy. I examined the
internal organs to see if I could find anything abnormal.
The liver seemed pale, and the blood did not clot, which
seemed peculiar. It was very watery and missing red

blood cells. I opened the bladder and found the urine to be red and bloody, a certain sign of trouble.

I saw Ken driving by, and I flagged him down. He stopped his truck, got out and walked over to the pasture. I wanted to ask his opinion about these calves.

I thought I knew what had caused the death of these heifers, but another view is always appreciated. "Don't jump to any conclusions," was his guarded reply. "Why don't you check the live ones while I do an autopsy on another dead calf."

Derrick, seeing all the activity, walked out to the field to investigate. "I need to have all the live animals rounded up and corralled," I told Derrick.

We herded them into a shed. I started examining the live calves. All the calves had a fever about 4° above normal. Some were urinating, and the urine was red and bloody. The results of Ken's autopsy were identical to mine.

I could think of two diseases that had symptoms of blood in the urine and high fevers. One was "red water disease" a problem occurring at high altitudes, in mountainous areas, and the other was Leptospirosis.

Lepto is an infection caused by spirochetes, organisms that look like corkscrews. When they move, they burrow into the tissue causing damage as they go. The target organs are the liver and kidneys. This would explain the pale liver and blood in the urine. Identification of the organism was crucial. A blood sample or finding the organism in tissue could identify our problem.

I phoned the Wisconsin State Laboratory in Madison to set up an appointment for them to run diagnostic tests on the dead animals. They said they would make time to work on these animals as soon as someone could bring them to Madison.

We loaded one calf that had been autopsied and two of the other calves that had died into Derrick's truck.

I am sure the lab people were not thrilled to have to incinerate these dead animals. Burning is the safest way to dispose of infected bodies. (A short time in the future, the Wisconsin State Animal Diagnostic Lab would only accept organ samples, and not the entire animal for diagnostic work.)

Ken had to leave because emergency calls were coming in, and I was left to administer treatment. I decided to inject oxytetracycline, an antibiotic, which I thought, might help. It is injected either under the skin, in the muscle, or in a vein. I injected the drug directly into the bloodstream of the calves that appeared to be the most sick. I treated the others with a shot in the muscle. None of them resisted the treatment or tried to get away from me. They were just too sick to fight.

I returned the next day to find considerable improvement in all the calves. None of the very sick ones had died overnight, and the ones with less severe symptoms were starting to eat again. I started another round of treatment, but this time, I had much more resistance from the rejuvenated calves.

I repeated treatment on the third day, and I was satisfied that these heifers were now able to control the infection on their own.

The lab called with the diagnosis. Leptospira was the organism that caused the death of these calves. Lepto is spread by drinking water contaminated by infected urine. There was a small stream in the field where the dead animals were found. The water in the stream must have been contaminated. We needed to notify the neighboring farmers downstream, so they could initiate a vaccination program to prevent spreading the disease.

Lepto can cause abortion. Often, the only sign of Lepto infection is abortion. The testing of blood samples after an abortion can produce invalid results, because the actual Lepto infection occurs long before the abortion. The antibody in the blood stream may have dropped to levels that are undetectable.

Derrick was lucky. We vaccinated his cows, and no abortions occurred. We repeated the vaccination in 14 days. All his animals are now vaccinated three to four times a year. This program has been successful in preventing new outbreaks.

A neighbor asked us to examine a dead cow several months later. We found blood in the urine, a pale liver, and thin and watery blood. I asked about abortions, and he said they were occurring on a regular basis late in pregnancy. "Hadn't Derrick contacted you about Lepto?" I asked.

"Sure, but I was too busy to take the time to get my animals vaccinated," was his reply.

I am glad most of the farmers have taken the initiative to vaccinate their herds for Lepto, because if any unprotected animals would get infected a new round of the disease would immerge.

44

Twenty-five years of practice was making me restless. Although I loved veterinary medicine, I felt burned out, and I wanted to do something else. Ken and I talked of me leaving and pursuing another career. Whatever it would be would have to involve some phase of veterinary medicine.

I answered an ad that had been placed by a small drug company in the Journal of The American Veterinary Medical Association. They were in the process of hiring a technical support veterinarian. I got a call for an interview. Ellie and I went shopping to buy new clothes for me. I bought an interview suit, a power tie, and a new white shirt. I looked good.

The interview took most of the day including lunch with the employees. Two things came out of the interview: One, I really did not want to be a technical support veterinarian. Two, I needed to work directly with cows and clients. An office job was not for me. I was not offered the job anyway.

The job was eliminated in just a couple of years when the company was bought out by a large pharmaceutical conglomerate. However, I still was looking for something different. The old routine just wasn't satisfying.

Ellie and I had been active in several organizations in the University of Wisconsin at Platteville. I had heard through the grapevine that the University of Wisconsin Platteville, College of Agriculture was creating a part time teaching position. They were looking for a veterinarian to teach animal science courses.

When I saw the 'position available' ad in the classified section of the Dubuque Telegraph Herald newspaper, Ellie asked, "Why don't you try for it?"

"Because I am not qualified," I replied.

"How do you know if you don't try?" she questioned.

And so I answered the ad. My interview would be in several weeks, because of the great response that had come in, I was told. Something like this made practice more interesting, and I was having fun telling clients about a new adventure, an interview at UW-Platteville.

The day of my visit to campus was one of those rare, sunny days that occur in late spring. The campus looked green and inviting. I made my way along the shaded sidewalks and stopped at the old building that housed the Department of Agriculture. It was one of the first buildings on the original campus site. UWP was a highly rated engineering college before it joined the University of Wisconsin system.

I headed into Ullrich Hall. Creaky old steps led to the first floor where the administration had offices. Classrooms and department offices lined a long hall. Students were emerging from all the doors and filling the corridors. I felt a little out of place and a little old. I made my way to the third floor where the interview was to take place.

I was asked to wait in a professor's office until the interview team had been assembled. He was on the phone talking to another candidate for the job I was interviewing for, or at least I was assuming that, based on the conversation. "This job is just right for you so be assured you will get it," he said into the mouthpiece continuing to praise the other person on the phone. He kept referring to the person on the phone as Doctor, and slipped the word veterinarian in part of the conversation. By the time we got to the interview room, I no longer cared about making an impression.

I was greeted by eight people some were professors, others lecturers, the dean, and the farm manager. The school had its own farm where teaching and research were being conducted. I was told that the job would also entail being the veterinarian for the farm. Everyone asked a question to start the interview. They were not hard or probing questions. I requested to ask some of my own questions.

I have always had a knack for asking penetrating questions that have many answers. I can predict what an answer might be and turn it to my advantage. Once started down this road, there was no stopping me, and that was how this interview was going. In the end, I was doing the interview. A short, predetermined job interview lasted three hours.

That night, Ellie and I had made plans to go to the Dubuque Greyhound Park with friends. I was late returning from the interview.

"How did it go?" Ellie asked.

"They will let me know in two weeks," I said, "but I have the job."

"How do you know that?" she asked.

"Trust me, its mine to accept or turn down," I said. We had a great time at the Park, and I didn't lose too much money on the dogs.

Two weeks went by, and the expected call came from UWP. The same professor, who I had overheard on the phone, called to tell me I had the job if I wanted it. His voice sounded subdued. I assumed he had voted against me.

147

Ken and I had to make a decision. Ken asked the all important question, "What do you want to do?"

"Teach," I said.

"We will need to hire another person," he said, and I agreed.

Now I had done it. My mother looked at me and shook her head. "How can you play with the big boys?" she asked. Some very prominent experts taught at UWP. Filled with self-doubt, I began outlining two courses, one for each of the semesters I was to teach. It took all summer. No direction or material had been supplied. I was on my own.

45

The job description of my new position stated that I teach three afternoons a week plus do the veterinary work for the University farm. I was assigned a 0.41 equivalent teaching position. Since I was going to be away from the practice for a number of hours each week, Ken and I needed to find another veterinarian to work with us.

Shullsburg Veterinary Service advertised in veterinary journals and at veterinary schools. Some people came to interview, but ultimately accepted positions in other practices.

It was almost September, and my part time teaching position was about to start. We received a call from a veterinarian who said he would be in town with his wife the following evening. He wanted to meet with us and discuss our advertised position. I wasn't optimistic. We hadn't been having any luck finding someone to work with us.

Ken and Heather had invited our prospective employee and his wife for supper at their farm. I met the couple at our office, showed them around the downtown area, and then escorted them to Ken's farm.

Dr. Bill Skog didn't look like a food animal veterinarian. He reminded me of John Denver, the singer. Bill had a physical problem. One shoe was custom made due to a congenital foot and leg problem. He walked with a limp. "This guy would never meet our needs," I thought. "He would probably find the work too physically challenging."

Bill's wife, Mary, had also graduated from veterinary school the previous semester and wanted to work in a companion animal practice. I was not aware of any small animal practice in the area looking for an additional veterinarian.

A keen mind will overcome any obstacle, and so it was with Bill. He knew he would be able to do the work without any difficulty. Ken and I offered him the job before the evening ended.

I think that Bill had made up his mind to accept our position, but he had to convince Mary. Moving to a small community would definitely limit the job opportunities for her.

He must have presented a good case. Within a month, Bill and Mary moved to the Shullsburg area, and I was free to pursue my new part time career.

A teacher must know more than the students, so I had to start studying again. I had found new reasons to kindle the flames of an old love. Veterinary Medicine no longer was boring, and the burnout I had experienced was disappearing. Teaching was a new challenge with new problems and endless possibilities for mental stimulation.

Classes were about to start. My enthusiasm for veterinary medicine had returned, but I started to worry about my ability to pass my fervor on to a classroom of students. Seasoned and savvy teachers are usually ready to meet their classes with a schedule and reading assignments. I met mine with butterflies and question marks.

I handed out my prepared materials. My ambitious workload was met with skepticism. "We only took this class because our advisors told us to, so don't make it hard," I was told in no uncertain terms.

"How about if we make it fun, and you learn something," I responded.

The first day was the hardest, but as soon as I introduced a case that applied to the outline, hands flew up with questions. My enthusiasm was contagious, and soon the class of eight students was enjoying my presentations, and more important, I was enjoying the students. My class and I bonded making my trips to Platteville fun and interesting

I had found a successful formula for teaching. Soon, word of mouth made my classes popular. My assignment consisted of two classes a year, one each semester.

The fall semester was a class on animal anatomy and physiology. Before I was able to find an existing textbook, I had to develop my own handouts.

The spring semester got a lot of attention. I offered a course entitled "Topics" where I took students on veterinary farm calls. The school provided a van that held 15 students. I held the class on my clients' farms and demonstrated the correct procedures for certain veterinary procedures.

I made students aware of potential problems. We used the University farm for a practical laboratory. The course became so popular that the university had to restrict enrollment. The first semester course became a prerequisite for the second semester course.

There was great client involvement in the "Topics" course. Mark Riechers, a farmer who raises cattle, had been a high school agriculture teacher. He shared his expertise with my students and showed them how he prevented problems by using new technology and ideas. Other farmers gave them information on how to detect sick animals. During instruction, I stressed prevention of disease. The class was unique in the University of

Wisconsin system. No other agriculture school offered a practical, hands-on type of course.

After 11 years, I retired from teaching. By that time, both courses were mandatory for animal science majors. I had more students than space. I suggested that we divide the students into two classes and offer both in one semester. There wasn't any extra money in the budget for increasing the number of classes. The school was trying to cut programs instead of expanding the ones already in place. The Agriculture major is now in a department within a larger college on campus.

46

Anaphylaxis means shock that may follow the administration of vaccinations and drugs. Vaccines and drugs have a caution or warning statement on the container or on the insert that describes what antidote is best to use in case of anaphylaxis. The antidote should be stored with vaccines and drugs. Unfortunately, antidotes must be checked often and replaced when they get old or discolored. Most antidotes are powerful, and when used improperly, can be deadly. Veterinary input on anaphylaxis reversal drugs is vital for proper use.

Often, repeated treatments or repeated vaccinations have greater potential to cause anaphylaxis. The immune system tends to recognize drug or vaccine proteins with repeated use and then defends against them by releasing histamines. The histamines cause the arteries to open and blood to pool. Not enough blood returns to the heart thus starving the organs and tissues of oxygen. This creates circulatory collapse, which can be fatal.

A milder reaction may be local, causing swelling around the vulva and head. Arteries open in the area and fluid accumulates. Allergies and allergic reactions fall into this category. If the fluid accumulation occurs in the lung it is called asthma. It is not uncommon to see symptoms between these extremes. The usual treatment for anaphylaxis is epinephrine or antihistamines. Atropine may also be a desired antidote so reading the label or insert in a product, becomes extremely important. It is too easy to grab a bottle of vaccine and not have the correct antidote available.

Most antidotes stimulate the muscles around arteries, increasing blood pressure, and insuring that enough blood returns to the heart. This reverses shock.

When I was in high school, I had an allergic reaction to an allergy shot. I had collapsed. I was in shock. My physician had to administer an antidote, and the shock was reversed.

Most antidotes stop histamine release. Blood flow is slowed; the fluid that invaded the surrounding tissue is reabsorbed allowing the swelling to shrink and disappear.

Keith Lane phoned with a big problem. He said he was vaccinating his cows for Leptospirosis. To his amazement, the cows that were injected were in trouble. Some fell as if shot with a rifle, others were breathing hard, but some others didn't have any unusual reaction.

I happened to be in the office when Keith called. I grabbed epinephrine and antihistamines from the shelf and rushed to Keith's farm. Some of the animals were recovering spontaneously as I would have expected, but others were still down and appeared to be dying. After verifying the correct antidote, I intravenously injected the animals that had the worse symptoms with epinephrine. I administered antihistamine to the rest of the cows. Now, it was a matter of time.

The Lepto vaccine that Keith was using contained animal proteins that caused his cows to become hypersensitive. He had used the same vaccine before and had not experienced any problems.

As I watched the herd for response to the antidote, Keith was pacing. Slowly, the cows that were comatose started stirring and moving their heads. I felt the elation that often accompanied the realization that I may have saved some cows from death.

I remained on the farm, and when it appeared that a cow was relapsing, I was able to counter its effect by giving more drugs. As long as the foreign antigen was available, relapses could occur. After a few hours of constantly monitoring the cows, I instructed Keith on what to look for and how much antihistamine to administer.

I returned the next morning to check on my patients and retrieve the medications that were not used. Most of the animals did not need retreating. Only a few were given more antihistamines. About 30 of the 50 cows were treated. None of the cows had died. This situation could have been a catastrophe.

Keith couldn't sell milk for about 5 days, but that was a small price to pay for what had transpired. It was no one's fault, but a side effect that can happen anytime when vaccines or drugs are used. Shock or anaphylaxis can be caused by any product that stimulates a specific part of the immune system.

The immune system can be of great help in protecting livestock against disease and other problems. Newer genetic engineered vaccines and other refined drugs make administration of these products much safer than the older products, which contained proteins from animals. In the future, drugs and vaccines will be designed to stimulate the immune system without relying on products that contaminate milk.

Even so, these new products will come with the warning, "May cause shock or anaphylaxis."

47

The morning started warm in prelude to a hot, summer day. The sky was cloudless, and the weather forecaster predicted we would have temperatures in excess of 90 degrees. My fertility herd check client for that morning wanted his herd health work finished early. He also requested punctuality; no coming late or doing other calls before his. Usually, I was able to accommodate him.

This morning was to be different. I had an early morning phone call from Mark and Michael White, brothers, who had a farm near Darlington. Ninety Holstein steers, which they had bought about a week before, were acting strange. These steers weighed about 500-pounds, old enough and large enough to make the transition to a new feedlot without getting sick. They had been vaccinated for all the routine diseases and were in good condition.

Mark and Michael owned many milk cows. They bought these steers to fatten on the extra corn that was not eaten by the rest of the animals. When they were big enough, they would be sold for beef.

One of the brothers was to meet me at the farm where the steers were fed. "This would not take long" I thought. "I'll be able to make this call, and my herd check call before the heat of the day becomes stifling."

I met Mark, and we made our way to the feeding yard. The yard consisted of a concrete lot with a tall wood fence, some nice pole sheds that offered shade, and a 5-acre dirt lot containing a small stream. The house was rented to a family that oversees the cattle for signs of problems. They had called Mark and Michael to tell them "something was not right with the steers."

As Mark and I approached the steers, we saw that most of the steers were lying down, and we heard a strange bellowing coming from them. When we forced some of them to get up, they would stagger off, but not go very far. We looked around in the buildings and found four dead steers. After walking around the area, we found three more dead steers on the bank of the creek.

Further examination revealed that some of the steers were blind. I think I had a diagnosis, but it just didn't make much sense. It was time for reinforcements. I used our truck mobile radios to ask Adda, our secretary, to send me some help.

Ken arrived first, and Bill drove in a short time later. We decided each of us would examine the area and the steers, and then, come up with our own diagnosis. There would be no talking among ourselves until each of us had inspected the animals. No one would try to influence anyone else until we all had a chance to observe symptoms.

After we finished the inspection, we all concurred on the diagnosis. It was lead poisoning. Where was the lead coming from? I had walked around looking for old discarded paint cans or discarded batteries, but I came up empty. I did find one can, the size of a soup can. It was riddled with small holes.

Bill decided to do an autopsy on one of the dead steers to see if there was any evidence of a lead product in the gut. He found some small metal granules that were unexplainable. We took blood and liver samples and had them delivered to the lab in Madison. The lab technicians promised us results of their testing by that afternoon. Bill and Ken had to leave and take care of other calls. I stayed on the farm to try to solve the mystery.

The steers were fed a no roughage diet, meaning that no hay was fed, only grains. This can cause peculiar cravings or pica. I observed the steers that were still up and walking around. I noticed they were continually licking at certain fence posts. I looked at these fence posts and found lead shot buried in them. How did they get there? Could lead shot cause lead poisoning?

I recommended that the cattle be moved away from this area. We needed to wait for confirmation from the lab, but I had Adda inquire about an antidote. EDTA is given because the calcium ion replaces the lead ion and helps in treating distressed animals. The cost to treat one steer was in the thousands of dollars and not feasible. I treated some with calcium gluconate, the milk fever treatment, but it did not provide any improvement in the condition of the affected steers. I left the farm as the steers were being loaded for movement to another facility.

I was really late for my next appointment, and Adda reported the client was not happy. She had called him, and told him that I was treating an emergency situation and would be late. The client still wanted the herd check, but he did not want to leave the cows in the hot barn any longer than necessary, which was understandable.

Later that afternoon, we received a confirmation of lead poisoning from the lab. I went back to the farm to talk to the renter of the house. He told me that he had been using the posts for target practice with lead shot in his shotgun. He felt terrible that he may have been the cause of the problem.

Moving the steers to a different location helped them recover. Some of the sick ones were permanently blind, and others suffered brain damage. None of the healthy animals became sick.

Mark and Michael hired a contractor to knock down the fence and all the buildings. The wood was burned and buried. A cornfield replaced the feedlot.

It has now been proven that lead, when shot into birds, can cause them to have lead poisoning. No-roughage cattle are more like single stomach animals and probably absorb lead faster.

48

Another feed mill has closed in our rural community. Feed salesmen were plentiful a few years ago. They were visiting dairies on regular routes. Some dealers would inspect a herd and then, comment on how their particular feed was superior to another brand. I would learn about these inspections from the client. The dairymen didn't like the competition, and I tried to be neutral. It didn't always work.

"My cows aren't performing at all," complained Terry Wallace.

"They are not breeding either," I commented as I removed a plastic glove in the process of performing a fertility exam. "Those cows that are suppose to be coming in heat have very small ovaries," I said. "They seem more nervous than usual."

"I noticed that as well. Some are kicking at me, and they don't like to get milked," Terry observed. Terry was a young dairyman, agile and small, making him a hard target for the hind feet of his bovines. Terry was also a fine dairyman who really cared about his cows and their well being.

"What has changed since last month?" I asked.

"Nothing I can think of." Terry replied.

Terry had a stanchion barn, the same as 90% of my clients. He fed grain and top-dressed minerals and vitamins in the barn. "Why don't we check the feed tags," I suggested. I looked at each ingredient and nothing alarming became apparent.

"Oh, by the way," he said, "since you were here last month, I started adding organic iodine to the ration. I was told it would create more milk," he added. "I didn't think it would matter since it is such a small amount," he said.

I looked at the numbers and did some mental calculations. I added together the percentage of all the iodine in the total ration and couldn't believe the results. "I believe we have iodine toxicity here."

All the symptoms the cows showed suggested that I was right, but I needed to look at Nutritional Requirement Council values. These are tables that provide the nutrient requirements of cattle. I went back to the office and found that Terry was feeding iodine at a level 10 times toxic values.

I called Terry and had him stop feeding anything that had iodine in it. Terry called back several days later to report that the cows were much less irritable. "O.K.," I thought, "this problem was solved".

Later that week, I received a phone message from the company that supplied the excess iodine. They invited me to lunch. "This, no doubt, is to thank me for finding the problem in Terry's herd," I thought.

The salesman and his manager met me at our office, and we proceeded to a local restaurant. "We are not happy with the way we were treated by Terry," the manager said. "He claimed we were responsible for his problems. You made us look bad. We lost a good customer because of you," the salesman added. "We think you are financially responsible," the manager said.

I was stunned. "Did you check the amount of iodine in the total ration?" I asked my face flushed with anger.

"Well, no," was the reply I had expected.

"Do you realize that the amount you suggested for Terry to feed is way above the toxic amount? The more he fed, the more you sold. Was that what you were trying to do?" I asked.

Both men looked at each other and then at me. "Nice day, don't you think," the manager said, obviously changing the subject to avoid any further discussion about their sales tactics.

About two weeks later, Gary Zoller called with a problem. "My calves look like hell, and some of them are dying," he said. Gary was an average dairyman, so I assumed he was exaggerating.

I drove out to his farm and was surprised to find calf hutches, good clean equipment and a very frustrated farmer. "You told me to get these hutches and the special equipment and just look at the poor calves," he said.

I had to agree. There were 10 calves, all thin with potbellies. "What are you feeding these calves?" I asked.

"You told me to look at fat and protein content," he said. "This milk-replacer contains what you recommended, but it sure isn't helping my calves," he said.

He was right. The tag, which listed the ingredients of the replacer, met the specifications that I had suggested. The calves should be healthy and in good shape.

"Have any died?" I asked.

"One died this morning," he said. The calf was typical of the others. It looked like it had starved, it's belly extended.

I began an autopsy by reflecting the skin and found no evidence of fat. Next, I opened the peritoneal or abdominal cavity. The stomach was distended and full, the intestine empty. I did not find any lesions, so I opened the thoracic cavity. Not finding any abnormalities, I opened the stomach. I had expected to see large milk clots in the stomach, but to my surprise, there was just a gray brownish mush.

I put my gloved hand into the substance, and it felt gritty and lumpy. The lumps broke in my hand. "Is there sand on the floor of the hutches?" I asked.

"No" he replied. "I use gravel."

I didn't find rocks or gravel in the stomach, but something that looked and felt like sand. I eliminated all sources for sand except the milk replacer.

How could I prove the milk replacer was the cause of the problem? We suspended a scoop of the stuff in water, and the sand separated from the rest. I had found the source of the sand.

Gary's face became red with anger. "I starved my calves because someone illegally added sand to milk replacer in order to make more money," he said in frustration. I remained silent, not saying anything, because of possible legal ramifications.

It took a long time for the calves to get better. The feed company paid Gary a substantial sum of money so no lawsuit was ever filed.

49

Our two-week European trip was a result of an intercultural exchange. Friends from Dubuque had become members of a worldwide exchange group called Friendship Force. One of the goals of Friendship Force is to plan exchanges between similar cities in different countries of the world. That year, Dubuque was paired with Guilford, England. Barry and Sheila Rudin, close friends, asked us if we were interested in joining them on this cultural exchange. I thought it would be fun, and maybe, I would have a chance to visit Holland. It had always been in the back of my mind to visit the country of my birth.

The schedule required the first week to be spent in Guilford, visiting our Friendship Force host and participating in the activities planned by them. The second week was available for individual touring. Ellie and I visited a travel agency and made plans to visit Holland and France in the second week.

All the Friendship Force travelers met at a parking lot in Dubuque where we boarded buses for the trip to the international airport in Minneapolis, MN. From there we flew to Philadelphia and finally on to England.

We were met by Friendship Force guides at Gatwick and taken by bus to Guilford, a community south of London with a population of 60,000. Our hosts for the week were to meet us at a central location and take us to their homes.

We saw Trisha Samuelson, our hostess, breathlessly sweep into the waiting area in Guilford. The coordinator introduced us, and we exchanged pleasantries for about 2 minutes. Then Tricia got straight to the point with a comment that she was late, and we 'had to get on with it'. Her son, James, was graduating from a private grammar school in less than 30 minutes. We didn't even have time to change clothes.

Trish, an attractive woman, was divorced with three children. The children's father was bringing James' two sisters to the graduation. Trish had an aura about her that attracted men like magnets. It was fun to witness, even though we were exhausted from our long plane ride. Men were mesmerized in her presence.

We toured the old school guided by the headmaster and were given a history of the premises that dated back to the 1600's. Imagine, just a few hours off a plane from the United States and attending a graduation in an old school that dated back to a time in history before the American Revolutionary War.

Trish's sole income seemed to be alimony. She owned a large, comfortable house with a lovely garden. She was always running a little late and had to 'dash off' somewhere. She worried her old car would just stop running someday, but she could not afford to buy a different one.

Her two daughters, Sophia and Katrina were delightful, very courteous, and polite. They brought us tea in bed every morning.

Her son, James, needed some male bonding, so he and I went golfing one day. I hit some balls on English turf. We became great friends. He liked his sisters and was extremely polite and open. We talked about his dreams and goals.

Barry and Sheila stayed with a different family in the area. The two families were friends. Sightseeing often involved the entire group, and we shared a lot of fun. We toured the headwaters of the Thames, which starts as a small stream before widening into the large river that wanders through the heart of London.

The weather was very warm for England and Trish decided to go for a swim. She removed most of her clothes and dove in the water of the tributary. She dared the rest of us to follow. The other men joined her, but I don't know how to swim. Trish knew how to have a good time.

One day, I asked, "Trish why did you consent to do Friendship Force since it seemed that all this intrusion would be hard on you? Why did you pick us?"

The answer was my profession. Her current l'amore was a veterinarian. She was trying to convince him to meet us. Finally, he agreed, and a date was arranged.

Trish was nervous all day. What if this meeting turned out to be a disaster? I tried to tell her that veterinarians talk about cases and problems all the time and conversation comes easy.

He showed up at the appointed time and after introductions we started talking. Soon, Trisha's friend and I were oblivious to other people and time. This always happens when two or more veterinarians get together. It was after 1 A.M. when he finally left with a promise to 'fetch' me the next day.

I was going to ride with him out to see English farms and dairy herds. He needed some advice on troubling cases. I was in my glory. Trish was thrilled that her guest from America and her friend were so compatible, and that he may get some free advice on his troubling cases.

Early the next morning, Simon, the veterinarian, picked me up to make rounds. The countryside was lush and green. Hedges marked the boundaries of fields and property lines. In the United States, we use fences made of wire. Hedges make the landscape much more attractive.

We saw cows that were somewhat over conditioned or fat. I think it came from the rich grass that was being fed. I was not able to help solve the problem cases that my friend showed me, but I gave him some advice on how to get appropriate answers. I think we both profited from the experience. I looked forward to telling my colleagues back home of my visits to some English farms.

Our week with Trish and her family ended too soon. It made us appreciate England, and its people. Someday, I would like to go back for another visit.

Our second week in Europe had been planned by a travel agent. Holland was the first place to visit on our itinerary. We had reservations to cross the English Channel on an overnight ferry that goes to Amsterdam. We had to take a train to the port where the ferry departs.

It appeared as though all the passengers on the train had the same harbor destination. The people were speaking Dutch, and chain-smoking. We were physically uncomfortable in the 'blue air' environment.

When the train arrived at the station, we got off and followed the crowd. They seemed to know where they were going. We had no clue. They were heading for a huge ferry that was right in front of us. Ellie and I lagged behind, because we had over-packed for this kind of adventure. Our luggage was slowing us down.

We boarded the ship, and Ellie produced our reservations. We were given directions and descended down, into the bowels of the ship, looking on all the doors and signs, but none of the numbers matched our reserved cabin number. I wanted to find our stateroom, because I was tired of carrying all the bags.

Finally, in desperation, we found the purser, who said our reservations were not for this ferry. We were told there are two boats going to the same place. Our reservation was for the ship docked behind this one, and it was getting ready to depart.

We had to scramble up the narrow stairs carrying our luggage. We finally got to the deck, found the gangplank, and hurried off the ship. We ran, as best we could, to the other ferry. The gangplank was being raised as we breathlessly arrived. They put it back down for us to board. That was close.

This was a much older vessel; not nearly as nice as the one we had just left. Our stateroom was extremely stark. It had a metal bunk bed and a small metal chest of drawers. The bathroom was small, old, and stained. I convinced Ellie we were only going for one night, not a week's cruise. We could tolerate that. We would be in Holland in the morning.

As the ship was departing, we went on deck to see the lights of the harbor disappear. We were in the North Sea, waves were crashing about the ship, and the water was very choppy. Ellie became seasick.

We stumbled back to our room. Ellie insisted on taking the top bunk, against my advice. I wasn't thrilled sleeping under her when her stomach was so queasy. We managed to sleep a few hours.

The ship stopped rocking early the following morning, which meant we were in the harbor. At 6 A.M. we heard a knock on the door followed by someone yelling, "Get off the ship!" No sleeping that morning, even though we both needed it. Hurriedly, we dressed, repacked and got off the ferry.

I was flabbergasted when I found out the ferry was not in Amsterdam. We were at The Hook of Holland and had to take a train to Amsterdam. Luckily, the train was waiting on the tracks close to the dock. However, it wasn't scheduled to leave for another three hours.

We finally made it to Amsterdam, exhausted and bewildered. The train station is a huge complex, serviced by many tracks. The mode of travel around the city is on trams that run on tracks. The tracks converge at the station.

Our travel agent had advised us to get a hotel reservation at the tourist information booth at the train station. We found the booth and were informed this was the busiest week for tourists in the history of Amsterdam, and all major hotels were booked. However, they would help us find somewhere to stay.

"Do you want a luxury room?" I was asked by the young, blue-eyed, blonde woman behind the counter.

"What is the difference between luxury and not luxury," I asked naively.

"Luxury means you have a private bathroom. Not luxury mean sharing a bathroom with other guests," she informed us in her lilting Dutch accented English.

We made a reservation for the luxury type room. She gave us directions for getting to the hotel on the tram. The tram would travel close to our hotel.

We got off in a residential area and found the street listed in the directions. I didn't see the hotel. This must be the wrong place. Now what do we do? Finally, I spotted a small sign jutting out of one of the buildings down the street. It said, 'HOTEL'.

The building was five or six stories high with steep cement stairs going up to the front door. We opened the door and walked in.

"What is your business here?" we were asked. The voice seemed to come from the shadows of the dark entrance.

"The tourist information center just reserved a room for us here." I answered, stunned by such a question.

"Follow me!" said the voice from the shadows. It was so dark in the hall that I couldn't make out who was addressing us. Once in the dim light of the stairs, we saw the person talking to us was a bent, old woman.

We struggled up the steepest and narrowest set of stairs I have ever seen. Only the front half of my size 13 shoes would fit on the stair step. I had to walk on my tiptoes carrying the luggage. We finally came to a door on the third floor.

"This is your room," the old lady squeaked. She opened the door revealing the interior of the room. I saw two army cots pushed together that made the double bed. The only light in the room was a bare bulb attached to a cord dangling from the ceiling. A large, unpainted, wooden box with a rod at the top was the closet, and a dirty, yellowed, pull down shade was the window dressing.

We walked in hoping it would look better once inside the room. Things deteriorated from there. The bathroom, which classified this room as a 'luxurious' room, was unusual, to say the least. There was a toilet and a shower. The shower head was slightly to the side of the toilet. There wasn't any shower stall or shower curtains. There was a drain in the floor, under the shower head. It didn't require much technical intelligence to realize when the water was flowing from the shower, it would splash and spray the entire room. Everything in the room would get wet.

We told the woman this room was not acceptable, but she said this was all that was available. We were exhausted, so we relented and decided to stay for two nights. Ellie was furious at our travel agent for not reserving a hotel room. We were in Amsterdam supposedly having a good time. This was a vacation. I kept thinking it can't get worse, but I was wrong.

Breakfast was included with the hotel room. It was very good, much to our surprise. It energized us. We wanted to tour Amsterdam and see the city we had heard so much about.

First, we decided to visit a shopping area. Ellie was not feeling well, her stomach was upset, but she did not want to go back to the hotel room. So we kept walking and looking in stores.

Unintentionally, we came upon the 'red light district'. Ellie's father had told us about this area. We saw 'gadgets' that made me blush. In the middle of this 'business area', Ellie said, "I have to go to the bathroom, NOW!!."

"Now?" was all I could stammer as a reply.

"Yes, NOW!" We picked up our pace, looking for a bathroom and finally saw a tavern. Ellie spotted the room with the picture of a woman on the door. She was gone.

I rarely go into taverns. I'm not a beer drinker. I stood there, sheepishly wondering what to do. Seven big men were drinking at the bar. A huge, 300 pound barkeeper was serving them. I thought the only thing for me to do was to join them. "I'll have a screw driver," I said because it was a drink I liked.

"Coming right up," he said in English. With that, he produced a screwdriver, the tool, from behind the cash register. All the patrons laughed and thought the barkeepers little joke on the American was very funny.

Next he came with a glass and ice. As he was mixing the drink, he was adding up the cost. "That will be 2, 4, 8 guilders," he said. I was reaching for my money when I overheard one of the guys at the bar commenting on how much I was being charged. The conversation was in Dutch, which I was able to understand.

"The dumb American doesn't know any better. The @#! $% Americans deserve to be treated like this," the barkeep said.

I wanted to respond and let them know that I understood what had been said, but I thought better of it. I certainly did not want to get into a fight.

Ellie came out of the rest room feeling better, and I timidly walked out with her. I left proud and thankful to be an American, but they would never know, because I said nothing.

I was anxious to leave Amsterdam. I wanted to visit Aalten, the city of my birth. We picked up the rental car we had reserved in America, and a map of the area and took off for the six hour drive to Aalten.

We arrived in Aalten in the late afternoon. We drove around the town and easily found our hotel. We were becoming smarter and had made a reservation before we arrived.

The hotel was a cozy, two-story structure, close to the train station. It contained a restaurant and bar on the first floor and rooms on the second floor. We were shown a small, dark room that was an improvement over the one in Amsterdam, but lacked amenities. Again, we asked for a better room. This time we were able to be upgraded to a large, bright, airy room, which was well furnished.

We unpacked and decided to do some sightseeing. The city had a population of about 15,000. Many of the people were bilingual, but the two languages were Dutch and German, not English. It was not a tourist area, but we were there to revisit my past. We actually met people who remembered my family. When people spoke slowly, I was able to understand them. They were patient with me when I haltingly replied in Dutch.

I found the house where I was born. It was a lot smaller than I remembered, but it had not changed. Seeing the house again gave me chills. The present owner was apprehensive and would not allow us to see the inside of the house. I don't think I would let a strange foreigner inside my house either.

The next day we rented bicycles and rode to the neighboring town, Winterswjke, where my grandparents had lived. I remember my mother taking me there on the back of her bicycle.

I found their house and decided to knock on the door. I introduced myself in my broken Dutch. The man who opened the door gave me a huge smile and spoke to me in English.

We were invited inside and introduced to his charming wife. They wanted to know all about my grandparents, since they were in the process of restoring the house, and wanted to have as much detail as I could remember.

There was the den, the room where my grandfather had held me on his knee. There was the dining room where my grandmother served delicious meals. The backyard had not changed at all. Pleasant childhood memories filled my mind. It was a wonderful afternoon.

We left Aalten after a couple of days and headed for France. We passed through Belgium and enjoyed a great view of the European countryside.

The highway ended at the outskirts of Paris. We had written directions, but were not able to find the streets that were on the directions. We realized that finding our way in an unfamiliar foreign city was challenging.

We knew we could find our hotel if we could get to the Eiffel Tower. We could see it, but when we asked for directions, we would only get blank stares. Pronouncing 'Eiffel Tower' in French is much different than it is in English.

Using my built in homing instincts, with which I find farms in the middle of nowhere, we did get to the Eiffel Tower and to our hotel. We spend three days in Paris, seeing the sights, and eating the good food. We had to use sign language to communicate and the little French/English dictionary that we purchased. The people were very pleasant and helpful.

Our trip back to England was a mere 45 minutes on a hovercraft. We said a tearful goodbye to Trish, and headed for our plane back to America. Our European adventure was over.

50

One of the most frequent non-professional diagnosis made by clients is pneumonia. Anytime an animal shows respiratory symptoms, the herdsman administers antibiotics. In the past, when Pasturella bacteria were thought to be the primary culprit of respiratory infections, the treatment with antibiotics seemed appropriate. The herdsman became proficient in injecting antibiotics to cows whether an animal needed it or not. It was a 'shotgun' approach to cover most respiratory infections.

Research has proven most respiratory problems are due to viruses that do not respond to antibiotics. Pasturella bacteria feast on tissue damaged by viruses. The bacteria are always present in the upper respiratory tract. These bacteria become invasive when lung damage occurs. Controlling this secondary bacterial infection with antibiotics gives the patient time to heal. Sometimes nothing can be done to help, and the animal becomes a "lunger," with permanent lung damage. The animal then acts as an incubator for more disease. Controlling respiratory disease can be a challenging task.

The combination of penicillin and streptomycin was used frequently by most dairymen in my early years of practice. Farm animals were given injections of these products at the first sign of problems, before a veterinary diagnosis could be made. Many needless antibiotic injections led to antibiotic resistance, and the contamination of meat and milk. I had to assume all animals had been treated with antibiotics before I had an opportunity to examine them.

One day, while on the farm of a new client, I visited the milk-house. It contained empty Combiotic bottles, the combination of penicillin and streptomycin. The empty bottles were stacked to form a pyramid that started from the floor and extended to the ceiling. I had to express my views on finding such indiscriminate use of antibiotics. My lecture was not well received. I was told my opinion was not appreciated and was escorted out of the milk-house.

When antibiotics are used for diseases caused by susceptible bacteria, a noticeable improvement can be measured in hours. In past years, antibiotics given at recommended dosage stopped the growth of the bacteria, and the animal regained its health. Currently, additional dosage needs to be administered to achieve the same results. When the higher dosage no longer works, a stronger antibiotic is used. Days of treatment are increased, and soon, normal bacteria needed to maintain good health are destroyed. The animal never quite recovers. More antibiotics are administered until the animal dies or is sold for slaughter.

Antibiotics should not be used to prevent disease. Prevention should be done with a proper vaccination program. The following case demonstrates that bacteria are not the sole source of pneumonia, and antibiotics cannot kill viruses.

I was on Joe Dobson's farm doing some routine work. Joe raised all the animals born in his dairy herd. Bull calves were castrated and excess heifers were bred and sold as replacement stock for other herds. Besides the home raised animals, Joe purchased feeder steers from local sale barns and co-mingled them with his home raised steers, a practice I considered unwise. "I always give them a shot when they get off the truck," Joe said. "It must work, because they don't get sick," he added.

"What do you use?" I asked.

"A long lasting oxytetracycline," he answered.

I didn't think Joe's procedure was the best way of handling new stock that was joining the herd, but he had been having pretty good luck, so I didn't say anything more about it that day.

On a beautiful fall morning, a few months later, a call came in from Joe. It was cold, and the first heavy frost was still in the air some clinging to fence lines and long grasses in the open fields. He sounded desperate.

"I got steers and heifers hardly able to breathe," Joe said over the telephone. "Come quick," he pleaded.

Joe had not exaggerated. He had purchased over 125 head of 600 lbs. feeder cattle, all in good condition. To these, he added his home grown stock that were the same weight and fed them in a group. All the animals seemed to be suffering, those he bought, and those he raised.

The majority of these feeders were thumping and breathing rapidly with their sides moving in and out in an attempt to force more air into their lungs. Others in the group had their tongues out, saliva and drool gagging them.

"I gave some of the bad ones antibiotics, but they don't look any better," Joe exclaimed. "I spent a lot of money on this bunch, and they are all going to die," he mumbled dejectedly.

I thought this could be my first case of BRSV, Bovine Respiratory Syncytial Virus. There was no way to prove it. Lab results would take too long.

BRSV or Bovine Respiratory Syncytial Virus is a fast acting pathogen that causes the release of histamine. It swells the microscopic linings of the lungs with fluid. The animal shows signs of asthma. In severely infected bovines, the appearance is that of drowning.

What to do? Thoughts of how to treat these animals were racing through my head. I needed antihistamines and steroid type medications. Should I use antibiotics? Joe said that they hadn't worked. I'll be selective and not use them on every animal, I decided.

Too much handling and crowding could cause such a severe oxygen shortage that some might die before being treated. "Joe, I am faced with a decision about treating the very sick ones," I said. "Crowding them may kill them."

Joe replied, "I can get a lot of help, and if we corner them with a gate and be as gentle as possible, maybe you can inject them fast." Joe replied. He had a point; automatic syringes work fast. "After we're done with one, we can use a marker on him," Joe added thinking of a quick way to identify the animals that had been treated.

"Great idea," I replied. Those not as severely affected could be caught in the head gate of our portable chute and treated.

A lot of neighbors showed up to help. The gate idea worked. Most of the severely infected just stood or were down and didn't move. The open mouth breathing that some were doing sounded awful. We treated all 125 head. I gave many of the very sick a diuretic to try and move fluid out of the lungs. With the marker, we identified the animals by the type of treatment administered.

Eight of the steers died, as their lungs continued to fill with fluid, and they could not get enough air. I treated the remainder for 4 more days. At that time, I determined additional treatment would not be of any more help.

Several weeks later I revisited the farm to work on an obstetrical case and asked about the steers.

"They are doing quite well now," Joe said. "All are back on feed and gaining weight."

"That's great," I said, relieved.

Joe had another observation. "There was no difference between those treated with antihistamines and antibiotics and those just injected with antihistamines," he said. "It was the antihistamines that saved my steers."

Antibiotics do not seem to influence the outcome of a disease caused by a virus.

51

Adda, our lifeline, friend, and co-worker was getting ready to cast aside the everyday responsibilities of maintaining the practice. She was retiring. In the past, whenever she went on vacation or on the rare occasion that she couldn't come to the office, she had found her own replacement. Retirement was not any different. She found us her replacement. In 1984, Mary Lou Wand replaced Adda Gehrt as office manager of Shullsburg Veterinary Service

Adda started working for us when we were just starting to build the practice. Because there was very little money, she had to use 'creative accounting' and juggle the bills. Some months, bills were paid to whoever provided the largest discount. Other creditors had to wait until our clients paid us. Time had a way of curing these problems. As the practice grew, we were finally able to keep current.

Fee collection was never easy. I am positive that everyone who could, would pay their bills. There were farmers who kept their accounts current, and Adda made sure we gave them first rate service. We had some deadbeats who never paid and were dropped from the client list.

Diplomacy was needed along with a good dose of reality, and Adda was good at both. She sometimes needed to diffuse angry clients who demanded immediate service. She often found the reason for their anger, and by the time the phone call had ended, the client had apologized and said he would wait.

Our office location in downtown Shullsburg is small and cramped. There was never a need to move or expand, since we did all our work on the farms we serviced. We had discussed a haul-in facility, whereby the client brought his farm animals to our hospital. It would have required a considerable investment and more personnel.

The system we had in place was working fine, so we decided not to expand. A few minor remodeling projects have taken place, but no major changes were ever planned.

The office remains as it has for years, a place for receiving calls, mobile radio service, and pharmaceutical storage. All ordering of drugs, simple lab procedures and preparing samples to send to other labs are done from this office. We didn't have separate offices for the professional staff. Everything was shared.

52

Rabies is one of the most dreaded diseases that infect warm blooded animals. This virus has been around a long time and almost always is lethal. For many years, 'mad dogs' were a common problem until vaccines were invented.

The virus has not gone away. Skunks, raccoons, and bats are known carriers. Some wildlife can carry the virus and infect their offspring without showing signs of illness. However, these carriers can get sick when stressed.

Researchers think that this virus may be responsible for some of the 'road kill' we see. Infected animals that do get sick wander aimlessly onto the roads and are not able to run away from automobiles

Human infections have resulted from people breathing the virus. Several cases of human rabies were reported in people who investigated caves. There were infected bats living in these caves. No human had been bitten, but some people did contract rabies.

Don wanted me to examine a cow that was acting strange. "What is she doing?" I asked over the phone.

"She's in a corner of the pasture acting belligerent, drooling, and wants to jump other cows," he replied.

"If possible, try to get the other cows away from the sick one. I'll be there as soon as possible."

Evening shadows were making their way over the lush green grass of Don Hansen's pasture as I pulled up to his barn. I could hear the almost constant bellowing of a sick cow. From my truck, I also could see the affected cow in the corner of the pasture. Fortunately, Don had somehow managed to separate the rest of the herd from the sick one. Don mentioned that the other cows seemed relieved to be allowed in the barn.

"I am afraid to go near the cow in the pasture," I said.

"I don't blame you," Don said. "Got any idea what's wrong with her?" he asked.

"I think she has rabies," I said.

"What do we do?" he wanted to know.

"We wait until she dies and take her head to the lab," I answered.

Working with a 'rabid cow' is dangerous because her saliva could contaminate an open wound. This cow was suffering convulsions and would attack anything that moved.

Rabies symptoms are described as having three forms: furious, being displayed by this cow; dumb, where the animal stares into space and doesn't move; and prodromal, where the infected animal appears normal.

Furious rabies is the most dangerous because of the possible injury to others, both animals and humans. Infected animals attack anything that moves or gets in their way. 'Hydrophobia' is the technical name used to describe these rabid animals. That's because they cannot swallow and have saliva drooling from their mouth.

Dumb rabies, exhibits some symptoms, but the infected animal is not aggressive. It just has a blank stare and will not move. These animals allow people to be near them. Handlers do not realize that the animal is sick until they try to move them. The virus can be transmitted through the saliva of these animals.

Prodromal rabies does not have any symptoms. There is no warning that the infection exists. It is always advisable to use caution if there is any suspicion of rabies in an area.

Incubation time, the time from the infected bite until symptoms appear, can vary greatly. Dogs are usually confined and observed for a 10-day period after being bitten by another animal.

Sometimes it can take two years before symptoms appear. It depends on how far from the brain the initial exposure happens. A bite on the face would have a shorter incubation period than one on the hind leg.

I left and returned to Don's the next morning. The cow was dead, lying in the same corner of the pasture where we had seen her the evening before. I carefully removed the head and wrapped it in many layers of plastic. Don's wife volunteered to go to the lab with it. Lab tests were positive for rabies.

We didn't know how many more cows were exposed. Vaccinating the entire herd was not cost effective; nor would it guarantee that other cows wouldn't get the disease. It might even change the incubation period. Don watched his herd for a few weeks. No other animals became sick. It appeared that only this one cow had been bitten by a rabid animal.

Pseudorabies is a similar virus. It has been a major concern on hog farms. Eradication programs have been introduced in major hog-producing states. Current knowledge indicates that the virus does not infect humans; however, dogs can become infected. There is no cure for them.

Constant bellowing and blindness were the symptoms first noticed by another client, Paul Zimmerman. "What's happening to my cows?" he asked as we walked into his corral.

"Tell me what you know, Paul; maybe we can figure this out," I said.

"Well, they were fine this morning when I milked them, and now, look at 'em," Paul replied. I was startled to see two cows acting in the bizarre manner Paul had described.

They would not stop bellowing. Their tongues were hanging out, and there was drool was all over them. Their heads were held high, and they appeared nervous and disoriented.

"I'm not sure what to make of this," I commented. "Let's see if we can get them in the barn."

Rabies was the first thing on my mind, but the symptoms were a little different. I began to doubt it was rabies.

I called my partner, Ken Curtis, for a consultation. Fortunately, his wife Heather, also a veterinarian was overhearing our conversation on the two-way radio. "What do you think?" I asked.

"Hang on while I check some texts," Heather said. She came up with a possible diagnosis. "Could you be dealing with pseudorabies?" she asked.

"Read me the list of symptoms," I suggested. The behavior of these animals fit the list of symptoms she had read. "Wow," I thought. This is supposed to be a virus that infects hogs. I hadn't seen any cows that were infected with it.

"Paul, are there any hogs around here?" I asked.
"The neighbor has some," he said.

It was getting dark, and couldn't do much more. I had collected blood samples and gave the cows antibiotics on the off chance that they might have a bacterial infection.

By morning, both cows had died. I asked Paul to check with his neighbor and see if any of his hogs appeared sick.

Paul's neighbor called my office later that day. Some of his pigs were in convulsions. I drove out to his place and found about 40 pigs that were affected.

Pseudorabies is a reportable disease, and I notified the office of the state veterinarian. The next day, I accompanied a state veterinarian to the hog farm to collect blood samples. All samples tested positive for the pseudorabies virus. The hogs were quarantined.

To protect the cows on Paul's farm, a fence was put up so that nose to nose contact between the hogs and the cows would be prevented. Eventually, the hog farm was depopulated.

This was my first case of pseudorabies in cows. Later on, I diagnosed more cases. The hog population on each infected farm had to be destroyed.

Cows in infected herds that had contracted the virus were not destroyed, because they are end hosts and do not transmit the disease to other animals. Cows must be in contact with infected pigs before pseudorabies can kill them.

53

Ruminants are important to man because they convert cheap plant material to expensive animal protein. Ruminants and man have shared a mutual relationship since biblical times. The animal supplies protein and humans must provide feed, housing, and care for the benefactors.

The way ruminants digest plant food was not understood for a long time. New and innovative methods have been developed that can aid us in providing the proper nutrition for these animals. Total mixed rations or TMR, systems are now popular. We no longer need an individual feeding program but can group animals together. This was not possible just a few years ago.

Ruminants have 'four stomachs'. Only one of the 'stomachs' digests food similar to other animals. The other three 'stomachs' are involved in breaking down feed to get it ready to be processed by the "real" stomach or abomasum. The first of the four stomachs is the rumen.

The rumen acts like a large fermentation vat. In it, bacteria break down the plant food consumed by the ruminant. Gallons of saliva are made every day. Saliva moistens, lubricates, and buffers rumen ingesta.

The breakdown of plant material by bacteria produces methane gas. Cows burp to release this gas during normal digestion. If the eructation mechanism, or burping, becomes paralyzed, the gas is trapped and bloating occurs. Bloating can be fatal and may affect many cows in a herd.

"Ya got to come quick, Doc or my cows are gonna die," Wilbur Thompson screamed over the phone. "They're all blown up like balloons," he shouted. Wilbur was about 65 years old and not easily fazed.

"Do you have a bloat trocar and cannula?" I asked.

"No," he replied.

The trocar and cannula is a pointed metal rod surrounded by a tube and is used to punch into the bloated stomach. The rod is pulled out after punching the assembly into the stomach, and the tube remains allowing gas to escape.

I jumped into my truck and drove to Wilber's farm as quickly as possible. I ran into Wilbur's barn carrying a stomach tube, bloat medication, a Frick's speculum, and several trocars and cannulas. A stomach tube is a rubber hose that is put into the cow's mouth and threaded thru the esophagus into the first stomach. To prevent the stomach tube from being bitten off, a metal device called a Frick's speculum is used to protect the rubber tubing.

Two cows were down. I stabbed both with the trocars, but only froth came out of the opening that was punched into the rumen. With a scapula, I made large, deep incisions on the left side of both cows. A large quantity of smelly, frothy material spewed out of the incisions. Since I was not able to get out of the way, I took a direct hit. The stuff covered me from head to toe.

"No time to clean up, Wilbur," I yelled removing my glasses. "Are any other animals this bad?"

Fortunately, the rest did not need such dramatic action. I passed the stomach tube into the rumen and poured in the bloat medicine, which would neutralize the gas and breakdown the froth.

Now that the majority of the herd was out of danger, I directed my attention back to the two cows that had required the drastic treatment. They had large gaping holes in their sides.

"Look at them," Wilbur commented. Both had gotten up and were looking around. "Want me to get my gun and shoot 'em?" Wilbur asked.

"No," I said. "I can sew them back up"

I cleaned each cow's skin and injected the wounds with novocain. I would suture the rumen first, and then the skin. As I worked, I asked Wilbur, "What happened?"

"Made a big mistake today," Wilbur said. "Turned these cows into new alfalfa." Most farmers know that new alfalfa can cause bloat.

"How come your 'stabber' didn't work?" Wilbur wanted to know.

"There are two kinds of bloat," I said. "One is called frothy, and the other is cavernous. Frothy bloat is due to tiny bubbles of gas that fill and expand the rumen. The buildup can continue until the animal dies. Cavernous bloat is a massive bubble. The trocar works well with cavernous bloat. When it is tapped, it goes down right away. To help animals with frothy bloat, we need medicines that break up the little bubbles and reduce surface tension. New alfalfa encourages bacteria to produce bubbles that are small and can't get out either through burping or my little tube," I said.

"I get it now." Wilbur said. "But what causes the other kind?"

"Well, mostly that is due to a paralysis of the burping mechanism, and gas can't get out." I said.

"What about the cows that are part bloated most of the time," Wilbur asked. "Seems like some cows walk around with too much gas in their belly."

"Those are chronic bloaters," I said. "They usually have a digestive problem that persists for a length of time. It either corrects itself or the animal dies," I said.

189

"Can anything be done for them?" he asked.

"An indwelling cannula can be used so gas can't collect in the stomach. It's like making a permanent hole in the side," I said. "After a while, the thing falls out, and the hole heals. It's hoped that the digestive condition corrects itself by that time."

My biggest concern for the cows I was suturing was peritonitis. If a lot of rumen contents remained in the abdominal cavity, infection would result, and my patients might die anyway. I used a lot of antibiotics both on and in the wounds. I injected intramuscular antibiotics and explained to Wilbur that he had to keep giving shots to these cows to help ward off infection.

Both cows were looking for something to eat as I left. I returned later that week to check them. Wilbur said they were fine. All I could detect was some swelling at the suture line. Both were ruminating and eating. "Good thing I didn't shoot them," Wilbur said.

54

Dehorning animals is an integral part of managing a dairy farm. The horns, necessary for self preservation in an era when cows were wild, are dangerous to domesticated animals and their caretakers. There are times during the dehorning procedure when arteries are exposed.

Jerry Clark called our office with a hemorrhage problem. "Got some bleeders with calves I had dehorned yesterday," Jerry said over the phone. "Two are staggering."

"I'll be right there," I replied. I grabbed several bottles of vitamin K, essential for the chemical reactions of blood clotting, and some plastic containers of hemostatic powder. The powder provides a dry base that expands the blood clotting surface.

The dehorning process removes the entire horn leaving a hole surrounded by an open wound on the top of the animal's head. A large artery feeds that area of the head. It starts above the eye and nourishes the lower portion of the horn. This artery then divides into branches to support horn growth. Another artery supplies the pole or top of the head and that part of the horn.

A December bone chilling wind was blowing from the North giving us wind chills of 10° below zero. The sunlight was muted adding no warmth to the already very cold day.

Jerry met me at the barn and led me to the heifer shed. Twenty Holstein heifers of all sizes stood in a group covered with blood. The older and larger animals had bigger wounds due to bigger horns. "We need to catch each heifer to stop the bleeding," I instructed.

"I'm way ahead of you. I have the neighbor's chute set up. Help is coming to get the heifers caught," Jerry said. "I even have a heater to blast hot air for your hands." My response was a big THANK YOU.

We started with those animals still squirting blood from the wound on the head. "I have had many animals dehorned and never had this problem," Jerry said. "Why with this bunch?" he asked.

"The blood isn't clotting fast enough for some reason," I said. "For example, molds could produce an anticoagulant, which interferes with vitamin K and the clotting mechanism," I suggested.

"I was giving them moldy hay," Jerry said.

"Other causes could be dicoumeral found in sweet clover and rat poisons," I added. They, too, interfere with vitamin K.

"So how does pulling arteries help?" he asked.

"Arteries are elastic and surrounded by muscle fibers," I explained. "By pulling them and allowing them to snap back they will tend to close and then seal."

"What if that doesn't work?" he asked.

"We cauterize the area with a red hot iron and seal it that way," I answered.

The horn wasn't cut deep enough, so with local anesthesia, I removed more horn material with a saw to expose the bleeder artery. The animals that had lost a lot of blood were given injections of vitamin K and an I.V. of saline as blood replacement therapy.

Pulling the arteries and treating all the bleeding animals took a great deal of time, but we were able to save all the animals. Those that had stopped bleeding on their own didn't require any special treatment. Hemorrhage that occurs inside the body is much more challenging and lethal.

"Come quick, Doc, Bessie has cast her withers," was the frantic call from Dick Sullivan. Dick was using an old phrase, which described a prolapsed uterus, a common problem for cows that have just delivered a calf.

Dick greeted me with a nervous grunt and frown. We headed into his dark barn where his cow was lying in a stanchion gasping for air and violently kicking her feet. A huge, expanded prolapsed uterus was protruding from her vulva.

"What's happening to Bessie?" Dick questioned as we approached the distressed animal

"I am afraid she just died, Dick," I said with a quiver in my voice. We had worked so hard to treat her infertility. Dick had been excited when I declared her pregnant. "She ruptured the large artery that supplies blood to the uterus," I said despondently.

"I don't see no blood," Dick said.

"I'll get a knife and show you what I mean," I said. I made a large incision into the prolapsed uterus of the dead cow. Big blood clots oozed from the cut showing Dick where the hemorrhage occurred. Dick stared with disbelief on his face. "I have had a lot of cows cast their whithers, but none have died like this," he said.

Blood carries oxygen to cells. When blood is lost in large volumes, tissues die from lack of oxygen. Hemorrhage, or blood loss, is a serious condition that needs immediate attention.

55

The MRI machine was banging in my head. I was captive and would not be released from it for at least a half an hour. I had been instructed to lie perfectly still, not to move, or the images would be distorted. The pictures were of my brain. Worry and discomfort were making this process very difficult. To pass time and divert attention, I focused on special cases that were either unresolved or just plain dumb. I decided on just plain dumb. An image of a big, mostly white, Holstein milk cow floated in my mind.

The cow, as I remembered, belonged to Fred and Homer Emerson who lived near Apple River, IL. Fred and Homer used our veterinary service only when they wanted to vaccinate cows because they are afraid to do it themselves. The automatic syringes allowed us to vaccinate entire herds quickly and for the most part painlessly.

I had two assignments that bright sunny morning. One was to vaccinate Fred and Homer's herd, and the other was to examine and treat a sick cow at a neighboring farm.

"You got time to look at a sick cow for me?" Homer asked after I had completed the vaccinations.

"I am in a hurry, but I'll take a quick look at her now," I said putting the syringes away. "I have an appointment with Chris Reed, your neighbor, and then, I'll come back and complete the examination and treat her."

"Doubt that you'll need to come back. We were going to let her die," Homer said.

This piqued my interest, and I really wanted to see what was wrong.

They took me to another building where I assumed all sick cows were housed. It was dark and gloomy. The cow they showed me was standing in a stall, looking depressed and uninterested. My examination revealed gangrenous mastitis. One quarter of her udder was dead and full of a smelly and toxic fluid. "She has gangrene in her udder," I said wisely.

"Anyone could have told me that," commented Homer. "I want to know what you are going to do about it." It would take time to treat a cow that was this sick, and so I again suggested that I go to the neighbors and then return.

"Don't bother," Homer said. "We don't want to spend any money on her." The silent Fred nodded his head in agreement.

"Really," I said in wonderment as I headed toward my truck. "Why is that?" I asked.

"Last one died, and she cost us a lot of money," Homer said.

I was mulling over the conversation when an unusual idea struck me. I didn't want the cow to die. Ken, my partner in our veterinary practice, lives on a small farm east of Shullsburg. He was making calls in this vicinity too, and we could communicate directly over our mobile radios. "Want to buy a sick cow?" I asked him over the two-way radio.

"What are you talking about?" he asked. I told him the circumstances and my idea. I would offer Homer and Fred $175.00 for the cow. It would come out of my pocket. I would pay all drug costs. I need you to feed and care for her, and we would split the profits. Ken reluctantly agreed and said, "I can get a trailer and haul her this afternoon if you want."

I drove to Chris's, treated his sick cow, and drove back to Homer and Fred's to offer to purchase the cow with gangrene. I was imagining she would be the first of a string of cows that Ken and I would own together. I planned to call her Adrian, a name starting with the first letter in the alphabet. Our herd of sick cows that were successfully treated would start with this one and then grow. I have an active imagination.

Homer saw me coming and asked, "Forget something?"

"No," I said. "I want to buy the cow with mastitis." The look on Homer's face should have been a warning. "I'll give you $175.00 for her," I blurted.

"Sold," came back Homer. Ken and I now owned a very sick cow.

Before I left, I treated Adrian with fluids and antibiotics. That evening, I went to check on Adrian. She stood in Ken's yard so depressed and sick that she would not move. Gangrene kills tissue, and the entire teat was blue and lifeless. I decided to amputate the infected teat. My scalpel did the job but a small portion of the teat must have had some live tissue because it started to hemorrhage. Blood was gushing from the incision. No one was home to help me. I had to stop the hemorrhage myself by suturing the wound. It took about an hour, but I managed to contain the bleeding.

The next morning I waited for Ken at the office to ask about Adrian. "Who," he asked? "You mean Crow Bait, don't you?" he added smiling.

"Oh, did she die?" I questioned dejectedly.

"No, but she might as well have. Yesterday, when I got there with the trailer, she wouldn't stand unless we forced her. Then, she went down again when we tried to load her. This morning, she can hardly get up. Poor move, partner," Ken said.

I wasn't ready to give up and neither was Ken's wife, Dr. Heather Curtis. Adrian had three veterinarians trying to pull her back from the abyss. Heather pumped 5 gallons of fluid into the cow's vein that evening. We both treated her with antibiotics everyday. Adrian didn't show any improvement. We decided that only Heather should continue treatment.

I had not seen Adrian in a week. Ken walked into our office and announced 'Crow Bait' would die that day. I was frustrated and disappointed that my plan did not work. I drove out to see Adrian one last time.

I expected her to be lying in the pasture, comatose. Instead, she was in a shed, very weak and moaning. I helped her on her feet, which took three tries. She wobbled out of the shed, hitting the door on her way. I thought she was saying goodbye to this world, but instead she found a lush clump of fresh grass and proceeded to eat it. It was the first thing she had eaten since I bought her. "You're not dead yet," I said as Adrian searched for another clump of grass.

Adrian began to improve and in the process began making milk in the remaining three quarters of her udder. Dead tissue was falling off the infected one and it was healing. Ken decided that if he milked her, he wouldn't need to buy extra food for his pets. Adrian began to improve everyday and was producing a lot of milk. The Curtis household was able to feed cats and dogs, a baby goat, and there was enough milk remaining to make butter. Ken didn't want to milk twice a day. This was a problem that we needed to solve.

I made an early morning call to David Wilson's farm close to Gratiot, WI. One of his best cows was comatose in the pasture and was about to give birth. I had told David about Adrian and the amount of milk she was producing on the drive to his pasture. "If you save my cow, get the calf out alive, and it's a bull, I'll give you the calf in exchange for the bill," he said. That was how Boyd came to Ken's farm.

Adrian adopted Boyd immediately. At first, excess milk from Adrian was still used for feeding cats and dogs. In time, Boyd was able to drink all of Adrian's milk.

Mother and adopted son were doing fine. Adrian had regained the weight she had lost, and Boyd was growing and getting fat. As time passed, the hot summer was giving way to the refreshing winds of autumn, and soon, the cold winter winds would descend from the north. "How long do you want to keep Crow, I mean Adrian and Boyd?" Ken asked, "I really have no room to house them for the winter." Ken added. Ken had a beef herd that needed all his barn space.

I went to Ken's farm to say my final goodbye. Adrian and Boyd were loaded in a trailer to be sold. We made a small profit on the sale, but not enough to justify doing this again. There would never be more sick cows bought because I thought I could cure them.

A quiet voice entered my reverie. "It's almost done." I was brought back to my current situation.

My doctor had ordered the MRI because I was experiencing tingling in my feet and legs. My feet felt numb. I had a difficult time walking. The numbness prevented me from feeling contact with the ground. The tingling and numbness had progressed to my face.

I felt confident that a minor circulatory problem had developed which would disappear after medication. "Just give me something to swallow, and I'll be fine," I had said.

"No. Get an MRI, and don't argue," the doctor instructed.

I went home after the MRI, changed clothes, and went to work. A few days later, the doctor's office called to set up an appointment. This was odd. Most of my conversations with my doctor were conducted over the phone. "I want you to see a neurologist," he said to me when I met with him.

"Why?" I stammered. He explained that the MRI found something abnormal and he wanted further consultation. "Let me see," I demanded. There, in the picture of my brain, was a white spot that wasn't supposed to be there.

Within the week, I was in the office of a neurologist. She reviewed the film of my MRI and wanted me to get additional scans, this time with a dye that was intended to highlight the lesion. She ordered more tests. Blood samples and spinal fluid samples were sent to the Mayo Clinic in Minnesota. I arranged for a follow-up appointment to discuss the results of the tests.

"Although some tests were inconclusive, the rest are positive for Multiple Sclerosis. I'll be right back to answer questions," the neurologist said as she momentarily left the room. Ellie and I sat stunned. Ellie hugged me, and I started to cry.

Multiple Sclerosis is a disease where one's own immune system attacks myelin around specific nerve fibers in the brain and spinal chord. Myelin is the insulation around these nerves. When removed, the nerve shorts out and often dies. The areas of plaque where myelin damage occurs show up as white spots on an MRI.

The doctor came back into the examining room prepared to answer the questions she knew would be on our minds. "How about my future. What can I expect?" I asked, still in a stupor.

"The prognosis is guarded because of your age but each person responds differently," she said. She suggested that severe MS attacks are treated with intravenous steroids. They can produce side effects.

"No thank you, not for me. I can live with the tingling," I stubbornly replied.

Ellie and I had scheduled a trip to Tokyo, Japan. Steve, our son, had moved his family there to enhance his job as an engineer for Caterpillar Tractor. I asked the doctor if I could make the trip. "Go and have a good time," she replied. "The trip will not affect your disease."

I continued to work until our departure. No other symptoms appeared. Steve, Lisa, his wife, and our grandchildren, Abby, and Hannah met us at the airport in Tokyo. I was tired, but so was Ellie. Our grand kids were a delight. We hadn't seen them for six months. They had grown. They hugged and kissed us, making Ellie and I feel wonderful. MS was forgotten.

The 'Japan Clan' took us touring to see the sights of Tokyo. We loved it, but I was having a difficult time keeping up with all the family members. They were so full of energy. Ellie hung back to support me. After an excursion, I would need to rest. I was still doing O.K. The neurologist had warned me that I would tire easily. Steve, teasingly, blamed it on old age.

Our return was uneventful, and I went back to work. The doctors continued monitoring and checking my nerve responses. It was getting harder to keep energized. I was starting to stumble. My vision became blurry, and I was struggling to keep my balance.

In May, 1997, I told my long time partner and friend, Ken, that I could no longer continue working. The initial symptoms arrived in February, 1997, and in three short months, I was facing the most unwanted decision of my life, forced retirement due to poor health.

The last farm call I made was to do abdominal surgery on a cow. I was feeling good that day and had gone to the farm alone. I prepared the cow, made my incision, and was getting another instrument when I stumbled and fell in the barn gutter, injuring my lip. I was bleeding and covered with manure. I finished the surgery, but it made me realize I was a danger to my patients and myself. I had to accept the fact the time had come to retire.

On June 14, 1997, my career as a practicing food animal veterinarian had come to an end. I could no longer walk confidently and felt constantly fatigued. It was impossible to keep my mind on my work. I was 60 years old and had practiced veterinary medicine for 36 years. I was leaving the job I loved to face an unknown future.

I left my veterinary truck at the office and slowly walked the four blocks home. Ellie met me at our front door and hugged me. Tears of sadness, frustration, and loss flowed between us. Suddenly, I realized that I hadn't lost everything; in fact, I had lost very little. I had the most important part of my life hugging me. Together we would fight this disease. I decided to phone the neurologist and start the intravenous steroid therapy the next day.

The true disease hadn't arrived yet. We were fighting skirmishes and losing most of them. The real battle was about to be waged.

Steroids are designed to lessen the effects of an MS episode by reducing the swelling in the brain caused by the lesions. Visiting nurses came to the house to administer the drug. They had a terrible time locating my veins.

I picked up on two important aspects of this disease as they described treatment. Everyone refers to what

what was happening as 'an episode'. Along with the symptoms of extreme tiredness and loss of balance, I developed a deep and consuming depression. I chose to spend my time in one room of the house; the beautiful 3-season room that we had just added the previous year.

I slept most of the morning, ate lunch and slept most of the afternoon. My eyes were failing. It seemed that the world had darkened, thus increasing my gloom. I needed support when I tried to walk. I kept looking for handholds. I had been overweight almost all my life, and now, I was struggling to eat. Ellie cooked all my favorite meals and despite all her efforts, I was losing weight.

For the first time in my life I felt hopeless and defeated. Sleep was a blessing. I didn't worry about the next day, the next hour, the next minute. When awake, I kept thinking what good was I to anyone. I was creating worry and anxiety to the ones that loved me, particularly Ellie. I knew I would never be productive again. I was angry, frustrated, and saw no way that my life would or could improve. The darkness became very oppressive. I didn't want to live. That's the real battle. That's the real MS. I was in a war, and the enemy was exposed. Nothing but my very existence would satisfy this villain. I felt myself losing, giving in to this demon. I had had enough torture and suffering. Ellie, my mate and love, said no. "I need you, I love you, and I want you. You are not giving in." I repeated these words over and over again. I could not allow her to be alone so I struggled on.

One morning, at the breakfast table, a brief, but wonderful event occurred. The morning sun was bright, and the outdoors gave off a fantastic light. For a few seconds, I saw the world again. The next day it happened again only longer. More then a month had passed, and I was regaining some vision. I was starting to walk without aid and beginning to gain weight. The 'episode' was finally ending.

The 'episode' left me with permanent disabilities. I have lost some vision in both eyes, but I can see well enough to read and drive. I have lost some hearing, but still am able to enjoy music. My left thumb has a permanent shake. I tire easily and need to lie down frequently, but now, cannot fall asleep.

After the steroid treatment, the neurologist suggested trying an additional medication that requires an injection once a week to help ward off new episodes. I regularly go to a fitness center to work out. I have regained most of my strength and feel pretty good.

So far, the combination of medication and physical exercise is working. I don't know what the future holds. No one does.